PARADISE AND POWER

ROBERT KAGAN is senior associate at the Carnegie Endowment for International Peace, where he is director of the U.S. Leadership Project. In addition to writing a monthly column in the *Washington Post*, he is author of *A Twilight Struggle: American Power and Nicaragua, 1977–1990* and co-editor, with William Kristol, of *Present Dangers: Crisis and Opportunity in American Foreign and Defense Policy*. He served in the State Department from 1984 to 1988.

From the reviews:

'Provocative... the most talked-about book of the year... *Paradise and Power* is energising to read.' Mark Leonard, *New Statesman*

'Kagan's book has already been distributed to every European Union ambassador, on the orders of Javier Solana, the EU foreign policy chief... In the European Commission it is read as a primer to Bush administration thinking. It is a rare achievement: a bestseller on foreign policy.' Julian Coman, *Sunday Telegraph*

D0109285

'The latest hot polemic exciting transatlantic policy types.' Jonathan Freedland, *Guardian*

'There have been plenty of books to look at the events of this year in a wider cultural and intellectual context. The one which made most noise was the academic Robert Kagan's *Paradise and Power*. The simplicity of its thesis – Americans are from Mars and Europeans are from Venus – was its great selling-point.' *Sunday Times* Book of the Year 2003

'Anyone looking for an intellectual primer to explain the geo-political forces at work in the Iraqi conflict should order a copy.' Editorial, *Sunday Telegraph*, 26 January 2003

'A compact and arresting book… A hard-hitting, unsentimental and yet liberal and humane manifesto… Highly readable.' Brendan Simms, *Sunday Times*

'Anyone who wants to discover how Europe's policy-makers look to Americans… should read this book.' Stephen Robinson, *Daily Telegraph*

'Kagan ranges over history and strategy, philosophy and economics… The Kagan thesis has become such a talking point because it offers an explanatory framework for the unprecedented bitterness of the transatlantic row over Iraq.' Daniel Johnson, *Daily Telegraph*

'Brilliant.' Harry Mount, *Spectator*

'Kagan's exposition of the European achievement is all the more compelling because he does not share its sentiments.' Johann Hari, *Times Literary Supplement*

'A book worthy of every thinking person on both sides of the Atlantic. It is hard to imagine so complex a subject being explained so clearly and so compellingly in such a small compass. What makes this brief book so important is that the author judiciously endeavours to see the problem from both sides. In an age characterized more by ideological axe-grinding than by intellectual fairness, that is no small achievement. Kagan is to be congratulated for a contribution unlikely to be equalled.' Gary L. McDowell, *THES*

'Kaganism is the doctrine that the Atlantic Ocean is much wider than we realize. History has lead to a fundamental and ideological division ... Kagan's project is not to judge these two positions, but simply to point out that the extent of the Atlantic divergence.' Bryan Appleyard, *Literary Review*

'Muscularly provocative ... Whether you agree with the book is not the point; what you cannot do is ignore it, wish it away or dispute its importance ... Impressive.' Alex Massie, *Scotland on Sunday*

'The ideal introduction to the current dominant position in US foreign policy.' Dermot O'Brien, *Irish Times*

'No piece in this realm has generated quite as much heat and interest since Samuel Huntington's "Clash of Civilizations" or Francis Fukuyama's "End of History".' François Heisbourg, *New York Times*

'Lucid and elegant... It is hard to imagine any future serious discussion of trans-Atlantic relations or America's role in the world without reference to this book.' *New York Times Book Review*

'Kagan is one of America's finest commentators on issues of foreign policy. He writes elegantly, has an excellent command of history and consistently demonstrates superior intelligence and insight... This book could not have been more timely.' *Los Angeles Times*

'Subtle and brilliant.' *New Republic*

'Truly insightful.' *New York Observer*

'Kagan writes with skill, erudition, and reasoned argument.' *National Review*

'This refreshing essay results from careful thought combined with critical information. Read it and you will think more deeply about this important arena.' George P. Shultz, former secretary of state, 1982–9

'The democratic West has divided into two: realist America, putting its trust in physical power, and idealist Europe, trusting to intellectual authority and multi-lateralism. It is true that, as Mr. Kagan makes clear, American foreign policy retains a strong idealist element, but it is its muscular willingness to act with force, alone if it must, that Kagan defends here, and convincingly.'
Wall Street Journal

'Brilliant.' *Business Week*

'I consider this one of those seminal treatises without which any discussion of European-American relations would be incomplete and which will shape that discussion for years to come.' Dr. Henry Kissinger

'Kagan's provocative and thoughtful essay is required reading for everyone concerned about the future of transatlantic relations... Although not everyone will agree with Kagan's analysis, readers will benefit from its clarity, insight and historical force.' Senator John McCain

'Ground-breaking... Robert Kagan's book will have a fundamental influence on how coming generations make sense of the world.' *Evening Echo (Cork)*

PARADISE AND POWER

American and Europe
in the New World Order

ROBERT KAGAN

Atlantic Books
London

First published in the United States of America in 2003 by Alfred A. Knopf

First published in Great Britain in 2003 by Atlantic Books,
an imprint of Grove Atlantic Ltd

This paperback edition revised and updated with a new afterword
published by Atlantic Books in 2004.

A shorter version of this essay originally appeared as an article entitled
'Power and Weakness' in *Policy Review* (June/July 2002).

1 3 5 7 9 10 8 6 4 2

A CIP catalogue record for this book is available from the British Library.

ISBN 1 84354 178 5

Printed in Great Britain by Mackays of Chatham

Atlantic Books
An imprint of Grove Atlantic Ltd
Ormond House
26–27 Boswell Street
London WC1N 3JZ

For Leni and David

PARADISE
AND POWER

IT IS TIME to stop pretending that Europeans and Americans share a common view of the world, or even that they occupy the same world. On the all-important question of power—the efficacy of power, the morality of power, the desirability of power—American and European perspectives are diverging. Europe is turning away from power, or to put it a little differently, it is moving beyond power into a self-contained world of laws and rules and transnational negotiation and cooperation. It is entering a post-historical paradise of peace and relative prosperity, the realization of Immanuel Kant's "perpetual peace." Meanwhile, the United States remains mired in history, exercising power in an anarchic Hobbesian world where international laws and rules are unreliable, and where true security and the defense and promotion of a liberal order still depend on the possession and use of military might. That is why on major strategic and international questions today, Americans are from Mars and Europeans are from Venus: They agree on little and understand one another less and less. And this state of affairs is not transitory—the product of one American election or one catastrophic event. The reasons for the transatlantic divide are deep, long in development, and likely to endure. When it comes to setting national priorities, determining threats, defining challenges, and fashioning and implementing foreign and defense policies, the United States and Europe have parted ways.

It is easier to see the contrast as an American living in Europe. Europeans are more conscious of the growing differences, perhaps because they fear them more. European intellectuals are nearly unanimous in the conviction that Americans and Europeans no longer share a common "strategic culture." The European caricature at its most extreme depicts an America dominated by a "culture of death," its warlike temperament the natural product of a violent society where every man has a gun and the death penalty reigns. But even those who do not make this crude link agree there are profound differences in the way the United States and Europe conduct foreign policy.

The United States, they argue, resorts to force more quickly and, compared with Europe, is less patient with diplomacy. Americans generally see the world divided between good and evil, between friends and enemies, while Europeans see a more complex picture. When confronting real or potential adversaries, Americans generally favor policies of coercion rather than persuasion, emphasizing punitive sanctions over inducements to better behavior, the stick over the carrot. Americans tend to seek finality in international affairs: They want problems solved, threats eliminated. And, of course, Americans increasingly tend toward unilateralism in international affairs. They are less inclined to act through international institutions

such as the United Nations, less likely to work coopera-
tively with other nations to pursue common goals, more
skeptical about international law, and more willing to
operate outside its strictures when they deem it necessary,
or even merely useful.[1]

Europeans insist they approach problems with greater
nuance and sophistication. They try to influence others
through subtlety and indirection. They are more tolerant of failure, more patient when solutions don't come
quickly. They generally favor peaceful responses to problems, preferring negotiation, diplomacy, and persuasion
to coercion. They are quicker to appeal to international
law, international conventions, and international opinion
to adjudicate disputes. They try to use commercial and
economic ties to bind nations together. They often emphasize process over result, believing that ultimately process
can become substance.

This European portrait is a dual caricature, of course,
with its share of exaggerations and oversimplifications.
One cannot generalize about Europeans: Britons may
have a more "American" view of power than many Europeans on the Continent. Their memory of empire, the
"special relationship" with the United States forged in
World War II and at the dawn of the Cold War, and their
historically aloof position with regard to the rest of Europe tend to set them apart. Nor can one simply lump

[1] One representative French observer describes "a U.S. mindset"
that "tends to emphasize military, technical and unilateral solutions to
international problems, possibly at the expense of co-operative and
political ones." See Gilles Andreani, "The Disarray of U.S. Non-
Proliferation Policy," *Survival* 41 (Winter 1999–2000): 42–61.

French and Germans together: the first proud and independent but also surprisingly insecure, the second mingling self-confidence with self-doubt since the end of the Second World War. Meanwhile, the nations of Eastern and Central Europe have an entirely different history from their Western European neighbors, a historically rooted fear of Russian power and consequently a more American view of the Hobbesian realities. And, of course, there are differing perspectives within nations on both sides of the Atlantic. French Gaullists are not the same as French Socialists. In the United States, Democrats often seem more "European" than Republicans; Secretary of State Colin Powell may appear more "European" than Secretary of Defense Donald Rumsfeld. Many Americans, especially among the intellectual elite, are as uncomfortable with the "hard" quality of American foreign policy as any European; and some Europeans value power as much as any American.

Nevertheless, the caricatures do capture an essential truth: The United States and Europe are fundamentally different today. Powell and Rumsfeld have more in common than do Powell and the foreign ministers of France, Germany, or even Great Britain. When it comes to the use of force, most mainstream American Democrats have more in common with Republicans than they do with most Europeans. During the 1990s even American liberals were more willing to resort to force and were more Manichean in their perception of the world than most of their European counterparts. The Clinton administration bombed Iraq as well as Afghanistan and Sudan. Most European governments, it is safe to say, would not have done so and were, indeed, appalled at American militarism. Whether Europeans even would have bombed Belgrade in 1999 had the United States not forced their hand is an interesting question.[2] In October 2002, a majority of Senate Democrats supported the resolution authorizing President Bush to go to war with Iraq, while their political counterparts in France, Germany, Italy, Belgium, and even the United Kingdom looked on in amazement and some horror.

What is the source of these differing strategic perspectives? The question has received too little attention in recent years. Foreign policy intellectuals and policymakers on both sides of the Atlantic have denied the existence of genuine differences or sought to make light of present disagreements, noting that the transatlantic alliance has had moments of tension in the past. Those who have taken the present differences more seriously, especially in Europe, have been more interested in assailing the United States than in understanding why the United States acts as it does—or, for that matter, why Europe acts as it does. It is past time to move beyond the denial and the insults and to face the problem head-on.

Despite what many Europeans and some Americans believe, these differences in strategic culture do not

[2] The case of Bosnia in the early 1990s stands out as an instance where some Europeans, chiefly British Prime Minister Tony Blair, were at times more forceful in advocating military action than first the Bush and then the Clinton administration. (Blair was also an early advocate of using air power and even ground troops in the Kosovo crisis.) And Europeans had forces on the ground in Bosnia when the United States did not, although in a UN peacekeeping role that proved ineffective when challenged.

spring naturally from the national characters of Americans and Europeans. What Europeans now consider their more peaceful strategic culture is, historically speaking, quite new. It represents an evolution away from the very different strategic culture that dominated Europe for hundreds of years—at least until World War I. The European governments—and peoples—who enthusiastically launched themselves into that continental war believed in *Machtpolitik*. They were fervent nationalists who had been willing to promote the national idea through force of arms, as the Germans had under Bismarck, or to promote *egalité* and *fraternité* with the sword, as Napoleon had attempted earlier in the century, or to spread the blessings of liberal civilization through the cannon's mouth, as the British had throughout the seventeenth, eighteenth, and nineteenth centuries. The European order that came into being with the unification of Germany in 1871 was, "like all its predecessors, created by war."[3] While the roots of the present European worldview, like the roots of the European Union itself, can be traced back to the Enlightenment, Europe's great-power politics for the past three hundred years did not follow the visionary designs of the philosophes and the Physiocrats.

As for the United States, there is nothing timeless about the present heavy reliance on force as a tool of international relations, nor about the tilt toward unilateralism and away from a devotion to international law. Americans are children of the Enlightenment, too, and in the early

[3] Michael Howard, *The Invention of Peace* (New Haven, 2001), p. 47.

years of the republic were more faithful apostles of its creed. At its birth America was the great hope of Enlightenment Europeans, who despaired of their own continent and viewed America as the one place "where reason and humanity" might "develop more rapidly than anywhere else."[4] The rhetoric, if not always the practice, of early American foreign policy was suffused with the principles of the Enlightenment. American statesmen of the late eighteenth century, like the European statesmen of today, extolled the virtues of commerce as the soothing balm of international strife and appealed to international law and international opinion over brute force. The young United States wielded power against weaker peoples on the North American continent, but when it came to dealing with the European giants, it claimed to abjure power and assailed as atavistic the power politics of the eighteenth- and nineteenth-century European empires.

Some historians have gleaned from this the mistaken view that the American founding generation was utopian, that it genuinely considered power politics "alien and repulsive" and was simply unable to "comprehend the importance of the power factor in foreign relations."[5] But George Washington, Alexander Hamilton, John Adams, and even Thomas Jefferson were not utopians. They were well versed in the realities of international power politics. They could play by European rules when circumstances permitted and often wished they had the power to play the

[4] Robert R. Palmer, *The Age of the Democratic Revolution: A Political History of Europe and America, 1760–1800* (Princeton, 1959), 1:242.

[5] Felix Gilbert, *To the Farewell Address: Ideas of Early American Foreign Policy* (Princeton, 1961), p. 17.

game of power politics more effectively. But they were realistic enough to know that they were weak, and both consciously and unconsciously they used the strategies of the weak to try to get their way in the world. They denigrated power politics and claimed an aversion to war and military power, all realms in which they were far inferior to the European great powers. They extolled the virtues and ameliorating effects of commerce, where Americans competed on a more equal plane. They appealed to international law as the best means of regulating the behavior of nations, knowing well they had few other means of constraining Great Britain and France. They knew from their reading of Vattel that in international law, "strength or weakness . . . counts for nothing. A dwarf is as much a man as a giant is; a small Republic is no less a sovereign State than the most powerful Kingdom."[6] Later generations of Americans, possessed of a great deal more power and influence on the world stage, would not always be as enamored of this constraining egalitarian quality of international law. In the eighteenth and early nineteenth centuries, it was the great European powers that did not always want to be constrained.

Two centuries later, Americans and Europeans have traded places—and perspectives. This is partly because in those two hundred years, and especially in recent decades, the power equation has shifted dramatically: When the United States was weak, it practiced the strategies of indirection, the strategies of weakness; now that the United

[6] Quoted in Gerald Stourzh, *Alexander Hamilton and the Idea of Republican Government* (Stanford, 1970), p. 134.

States is powerful, it behaves as powerful nations do. When the European great powers were strong, they believed in strength and martial glory. Now they see the world through the eyes of weaker powers. These very different points of view have naturally produced differing strategic judgments, differing assessments of threats and of the proper means of addressing them, different calculations of interest, and differing perspectives on the value and meaning of international law and international institutions.

But even the power gap offers only part of the explanation for the broad gulf that has opened between the United States and Europe. For along with these natural consequences of the transatlantic disparity of power, there has also opened a broad ideological gap. Europeans, because of their unique historical experience of the past century—culminating in the creation of the European Union—have developed a set of ideals and principles regarding the utility and morality of power different from the ideals and principles of Americans, who have not shared that experience. If the strategic chasm between the United States and Europe appears greater than ever today, and grows still wider at a worrying pace, it is because these material and ideological differences reinforce one another. The divisive trend they together produce may be impossible to reverse.

THE POWER GAP

Some might ask, what is new? It is true that Europe has been declining as a global military power for a long time. The most damaging blow to both European power and confidence fell almost a century ago, in the world war that broke out in 1914. That horrendous conflict devastated three of the five European powers—Germany, Austria-Hungary, and Russia—that had been key pillars of the continental balance of power since 1871. It damaged European economies, forcing them into decades-long dependence on American bankers. But most of all, the war destroyed the will and spirit of Great Britain and France, at least until the British rallied under Churchill in 1939, when it was too late to avoid another world war. In the 1920s, Britain reeled from the "senseless" slaughter of a whole generation of young men at Passchendaele and other killing fields, and the British government began at war's end the rapid demobilization of its army. A frightened France had struggled to maintain adequate military force to deter what it considered the inevitable return of German power and revanchism. In the early 1920s, France was desperate for an alliance with Great Britain, but the Anglo-American guarantee to defend France stipulated in the Versailles Treaty vanished into thin air when the U.S. Senate refused to ratify it. Meanwhile, the traumatized British, somehow convincing themselves against all reason that France, not Germany, was the greatest threat to European peace, proceeded to insist, as late as 1934, that France disarm itself to the level of Germany. Winston Churchill's was a lonely voice warning of the "awful danger" of "perpetually asking the French to weaken themselves."[7]

The interwar era was Europe's first attempt to move beyond power politics, to make a virtue out of weakness. Instead of relying on power, as they had in the past, the European victors in World War I put their faith in "collective security" and in its institutional embodiment, the League of Nations. "Our purpose," declared one of the league's leading statesmen, was "to make war impossible, to kill it, to annihilate it. To do this we had to create a system."[8] But the "system" did not work, in part because its leading members had neither the power nor the will. It is ironic that the driving intellectual force behind this effort to solve Europe's security crisis through the creation of a supranational legal institution was an American, Woodrow Wilson. Wilson spoke with the authority of what had in recent decades become one of the world's richest and most powerful countries, and whose late entry into World War I had significantly aided the Allied victory. Unfortunately, Wilson spoke for America at a time when it, too, was running away from power, and, as it turned out, he did not actually speak for his country. The American refusal to participate in the institution Wilson created destroyed whatever small chance it may have had to succeed. As Churchill wryly recalled, "We, who had deferred so much to [Wilson's] opinions and wishes in all this busi-

[7] Winston Churchill, *The Gathering Storm* (Boston, 1948), p. 94.

[8] Edvard Benes quoted in E. H. Carr, *The Twenty Years' Crisis, 1919–1939* (London, 1948), p. 30.

ness of peacemaking, were told without much ceremony that we ought to be better informed about the American Constitution."[9] The Europeans were left to themselves, and when confronted by the rising power of a rearming, revisionist Germany in the 1930s, "collective security" melted away and was replaced by the policy of appeasement.

At its core, the appeasement of Nazi Germany was a strategy based on weakness, which derived less from genuine inability to contain German power than from the understandable fear of another great European war. But built on top of this foundation was an elaborate structure of sophisticated arguments about the nature of the threat posed by Germany and the best means of addressing it. British officials, in particular, consistently downplayed the threat, or insisted that it was not yet serious enough to require action. "If it could be proved that Germany was rearming," the British Conservative leader Stanley Baldwin said in 1933, then Europe would have to do something. "But that situation had not yet arisen."[10] Proponents of appeasement produced many reasons why the application of power was unnecessary or inappropriate. Some argued that Germany and its Nazi government had legitimate grievances that had to be taken into account by the Western powers. The Versailles Treaty, as John Maynard Keynes explained, had been harsh and counterproductive, and Britain and France had only themselves to blame if Ger-

[9] Churchill, *The Gathering Storm*, p. 12.

[10] Quoted in A. J. P. Taylor, *The Origins of the Second World War* (New York, 1983), pp. 73–74.

man politics had turned angry and revanchist. When Hitler complained about the mistreatment of ethnic Germans in Czechoslovakia and elsewhere, the Western democracies were prepared to concede the point. Nor did the other European powers want to believe that an ideological rift made compromise with Hitler and the Nazis impossible. In 1936 the French prime minister, Léon Blum, told a visiting German minister, "I am a Marxist and a Jew," but "we cannot achieve anything if we treat ideological barriers as insurmountable."[11] Many convinced themselves that although Hitler seemed bad, the alternatives to him in Germany were probably worse. British and French officials worked to gain Hitler's signature on agreements, believing he alone could control what were assumed to be the more extreme forces in German society.[12]

The purpose of appeasement was to buy time and hope that Hitler could be satisfied. But the strategy proved disastrous for Britain and France. Every passing year allowed Germany to exploit its latent economic and industrial superiority and to rearm, to the point where the democratic European powers were incapable of deterring or defeating Hitler when he finally struck. In 1940, Hitler's minister of propaganda, Joseph Goebbels, looked back on

[11] Quoted in Henry Kissinger, *Diplomacy* (New York, 1994), p. 307.

[12] As one French official stationed in Berlin put it, "If Hitler is sincere in proclaiming his desire for peace, we will be able to congratulate ourselves on having reached agreement; if he has other designs or if he has to give way one day to some fanatic we will at least have postponed the outbreak of a war and that is indeed a gain." Quoted in Anthony Adamthwaite, *France and the Coming of the Second World War, 1936–1939* (London, 1977), p. 30; Kissinger, *Diplomacy*, p. 294.

the previous two decades of European diplomacy with some amazement.

> In 1933 a French premier ought to have said (and if I had been the French premier I would have said it): "The new Reich Chancellor is the man who wrote *Mein Kampf,* which says this and that. This man cannot be tolerated in our vicinity. Either he disappears or we march!" But they didn't do it. They left us alone and let us slip through the risky zone, and we were able to sail around all dangerous reefs. *And when we were done, and well armed, better than they, then they started the war!*[13]

The sophisticated arguments of appeasement might conceivably have been more valid had they been applied to a different man and a different country under different circumstances—for instance, to the German leader of the 1920s, Gustav Stresemann. They had been misapplied to Hitler and the Germany of the 1930s. But then, in truth, the appeasement strategy had been a product not of analysis but of weakness.

If World War I severely weakened Europe, the Second World War that resulted from this failure of European strategy and diplomacy all but destroyed European nations as global powers. Their postwar inability to project sufficient force overseas to maintain colonial empires in Asia, Africa, and the Middle East forced them to retreat

---

[13] Quoted in Paul Johnson, *Modern Times: The World from the Twenties to the Eighties* (New York, 1983), p. 341.

on a massive scale after more than five centuries of imperial dominance—perhaps the most significant retrench-
ment of global influence in human history. Less than a
decade into the Cold War, Europeans ceded both colonial
holdings and strategic responsibilities in Asia and the
Middle East to the United States, sometimes willingly and
sometimes under American pressure, as in the Suez crisis.

At the end of World War II, many influential Americans had hoped that Europe could be reestablished as a
"third force" in the world, strong enough to hold its own
against the Soviet Union and allow the United States to
pull back from Europe. Franklin Roosevelt, Dean Acheson, and other American observers believed Great Britain
would shoulder the burden of defending much of the
world against the Soviet Union. In those early postwar
days, President Harry Truman could even imagine a world
where London and Moscow competed for influence, with
the United States serving as "an impartial umpire."[14] But
then the British government made clear that it could not
continue the economic and military support to Greece
and Turkey it had been providing since the end of the war.
By 1947, British officials saw that the United States would
soon be "plucking the torch of world leadership from
our chilling hands."[15] Europe was now dependent on the
United States for its own security and for global security.
France and Britain did not even like the idea of an independent European bloc, a "third force," fearing it would
provide the excuse for American withdrawal from Europe.

[14] John Lewis Gaddis, *The Long Peace* (New York, 1987), p. 55.
[15] Ibid.

Once again they would be left alone facing Germany, and now the Soviet Union as well. As one American official put it, "The one faint element of confidence which [the French] cling to is the fact that American troops, however strong in number, stand between them and the Red Army."[16]

From the end of World War II and for the next fifty years, therefore, Europe fell into a state of strategic dependence on the United States. The once global reach of the European powers no longer extended beyond the Continent. Europe's sole, if vital, strategic mission during the Cold War was to stand firm and defend its own territory against any Soviet offensive until the Americans arrived. And Europeans were hard pressed to do even that. European unwillingness to spend as much on their military as American administrations believed necessary was a constant source of transatlantic tension, from the establishment of NATO to the days of Kennedy, whose doctrine of "flexible response" depended on a significant increase in European conventional forces, to the Reagan years, when American congressmen clamored for Europe to do more to "share the burden" of the common defense.

But the circumstances of the Cold War created a perhaps unavoidable tension between American and European interests. Americans generally preferred an effective European military capability—under NATO control, of course—that could stop Soviet armies on European soil short of nuclear war and with the bulk of casualties suffered by Europeans, not Americans. Not surprisingly, many

[16] Quoted in ibid., p. 65

Europeans took a different view of the most desirable form of deterrence. They were content to rely on the protection offered by the U.S. nuclear umbrella, hoping that Europe's safety could be preserved by the U.S.-Soviet balance of terror and the doctrine of mutually assured destruction. In the early years of the Cold War, European economies were too weak to build up sufficient military capacity for self-defense anyway. But even when European economies recovered later in the Cold War, the Europeans were not especially interested in closing the military gap. The American nuclear guarantee deprived Europeans of the incentive to spend the kind of money that would have been necessary to restore them to military great-power status. This psychology of dependence was also an unavoidable reality of the Cold War and the nuclear age. A proud Gaullist France might try to escape it by leaving NATO and building its own small nuclear force. But the *force de frappe* was little more than symbolism; it relieved neither France nor Europe from strategic dependence on the United States.

If Europe's relative weakness appeared less of a problem in transatlantic relations during the Cold War, it was partly because of the unique geopolitical circumstances of that conflict. Although dwarfed by the two superpowers on its flanks, a weakened Europe nevertheless served as the central strategic theater of the worldwide struggle between communism and democratic capitalism, and this, along with lingering habits of world leadership, allowed Europeans to retain international influence and international respect beyond what their sheer military capabilities might have afforded. America's Cold War strategy was built around the transatlantic alliance. Maintaining the unity and cohesion of "the West" was essential. Naturally, this elevated the importance of European opinion on global matters, giving both Europeans and Americans a perhaps exaggerated estimation of European power.

The perception persisted into the 1990s. The Balkan conflicts of that decade forced the United States to continue attending to Europe as a strategic priority. The NATO alliance appeared to have found a new, post–Cold War mission in bringing peace to that part of the Continent still prone to violent ethnic conflict, which, though on a smaller scale, appeared not unlike the century's earlier great conflicts. The enlargement of the NATO alliance to include former members of the Soviet bloc—the completion of the Cold War victory and the creation of a Europe "whole and free"—was another grand project of the West that kept Europe in the forefront of American political and strategic thinking.

And then there was the early promise of the "new" Europe. By bonding together into a single political and economic unit—the historic accomplishment of Maastricht in 1992—many hoped to recapture Europe's old greatness in a new political form. "Europe" would be the next superpower, not only economically and politically but also militarily. It would handle crises on the European continent, such as the ethnic conflicts in the Balkans, and it would reemerge as a global player of the first rank. In the 1990s, Europeans could still confidently assert that the power of a unified Europe would restore, finally, the global "multipolarity" that had been destroyed by the Cold War and its aftermath. And most Americans, with mixed emotions, agreed that superpower Europe was the future. Harvard University's Samuel P. Huntington predicted that the coalescing of the European Union would be "the single most important move" in a worldwide reaction against American hegemony and would produce a "truly multipolar" twenty-first century.[17]

Had Europe fulfilled this promise during the 1990s, the world would probably be a different place today. The United States and Europe might now be negotiating the new terms of a relationship based on a rough equality of power, instead of struggling with their vast disparity. It is possible that the product of that mutual adjustment would have been beneficial to both sides, with Europe taking on some of the burdens of global security and the United States paying greater deference to European interests and aspirations as it formulated its own foreign policies.

But the "new" Europe did not fulfill this promise. In the economic and political realms, the European Union produced miracles. Despite the hopes and fears of skeptics on both sides of the Atlantic, Europe made good on the promise of unity. And the united Europe emerged as an economic power of the first rank, able to hold its own with the United States and the Asian economies and to negotiate matters of international trade and finance on equal terms. If the end of the Cold War had ushered in an era where economic power mattered more than military power, as many in both Europe and the United States had

[17] Samuel P. Huntington, "The Lonely Superpower," *Foreign Affairs* 78 (March/April 1999): 35–49.

expected it would, then the European Union would indeed have been poised to shape the world order with as much influence as the United States. But the end of the Cold War did not reduce the salience of military power, and Europeans discovered that economic power did not necessarily translate into strategic and geopolitical power. The United States, which remained both an economic and a military giant, far outstripped Europe in the total power it could bring to bear on the international scene.

In fact, the 1990s witnessed not the rise of a European superpower but the further decline of Europe into relative military weakness compared to the United States. The Balkan conflict at the beginning of the decade revealed European military incapacity and political disarray; the Kosovo conflict at decade's end exposed a transatlantic gap in military technology and the ability to wage modern warfare that would only widen in subsequent years. Outside of Europe, by the close of the 1990s, the disparity was even more starkly apparent as it became clear that the ability and will of European powers, individually or collectively, to project decisive force into regions of conflict beyond the Continent were negligible. Europeans could provide peacekeeping forces in the Balkans—indeed, they eventually did provide the vast bulk of those forces in Bosnia, Kosovo, and Macedonia—and even in Afghanistan and perhaps someday in Iraq. But they lacked the wherewithal to introduce and sustain a fighting force in potentially hostile territory, even in Europe. Under the best of circumstances, the European role was limited to filling out peacekeeping forces after the United States had, largely on its own, carried out the decisive phases of a military mission and stabilized the situation. As some Europeans put it, the real division of labor consisted of the United States "making the dinner" and the Europeans "doing the dishes."

A greater American propensity to use military force did not always mean a greater willingness to risk casualties. The disparity in military capability had nothing to do with the relative courage of American and European soldiers. If anything, French and British and even German governments could sometimes be less troubled by the risks to their troops than were American presidents. During the Balkan crisis in the mid-1990s and later in Kosovo, British Prime Minister Tony Blair was more willing to put forces on the ground against Serbia than was President Bill Clinton. But in some ways this disparity, too, worked against the Europeans. The American desire to avoid casualties and the American willingness to spend heavily on new military technologies provided the United States with a formidable military capability that gave it deadly accuracy from great distances with lower risk to forces. European militaries, on the other hand, were less technologically advanced and more dependent on troops fighting in closer quarters. The effect of this technological gap, which opened wide over the course of the 1990s, when the U.S. military made remarkable advances in precision-guided munitions, joint-strike operations, and communications and intelligence gathering, only made Americans even more willing to go to war than Europeans, who lacked the ability to launch devastating attacks from safer distances and therefore had to pay a bigger price for launching any attack at all.

These European military inadequacies compared to the power of the United States should have come as no surprise, since these were characteristics of European forces during the Cold War. The strategic challenge of the Cold War and of a containment doctrine that required, in George Kennan's famous words, "adroit and vigilant counter-force at a series of constantly shifting geographical and political points" had compelled the United States to build a military force capable of projecting power into several distant regions at once.[18] Europe's strategic role had been entirely different, to defend itself and withstand the onslaught of Soviet forces, not to project power.[19] For most European powers, this required maintaining large land forces ready to block Soviet invasion routes in their own territory, not mobile forces capable of being shipped to distant regions. Americans and Europeans who proposed after the Cold War that Europe should expand its strategic role beyond the Continent were asking for a revolutionary shift in European strategy and capability. It was unrealistic to expect Europeans to return to the international great-power status they had enjoyed prior to World War II, unless European peoples were willing to shift significant resources from social to military programs and to restructure and modernize their militaries to replace

[18] X [George F. Kennan], "The Sources of Soviet Conduct," *Foreign Affairs*, July 1947, reprinted in James F. Hoge Jr. and Fareed Zakaria, eds., *The American Encounter: The United States and the Making of the Modern World* (New York, 1997), p. 165.

[19] The United Kingdom and France had the greatest capability to project force overseas, but their capacity was much smaller than that of the United States.

forces designed for passive territorial defense with forces capable of being delivered and sustained far from home.

Clearly, European voters were not willing to make such a revolutionary shift in priorities. Not only were they unwilling to pay to project force beyond Europe, but, after the Cold War, they would not pay for sufficient force to conduct even minor military actions on their own continent without American help. Nor did it seem to matter whether European publics were being asked to spend money to strengthen NATO or an independent European foreign and defense policy. Their answer was the same. Rather than viewing the collapse of the Soviet Union as an opportunity to expand Europe's strategic purview, Europeans took it as an opportunity to cash in on a sizable peace dividend. For Europe, the fall of the Soviet Union did not just eliminate a strategic adversary; in a sense, it eliminated the need for geopolitics. Many Europeans took the end of the Cold War as a holiday from strategy. Despite talk of establishing Europe as a global superpower, therefore, average European defense budgets gradually fell below 2 percent of GDP, and throughout the 1990s, European military capabilities steadily fell behind those of the United States.

The end of the Cold War had a different effect on the other side of the Atlantic. For although Americans looked for a peace dividend, too, and defense budgets declined or remained flat during most of the 1990s, defense spending still remained above 3 percent of GDP. Fast on the heels of the Soviet empire's demise came Iraq's invasion of Kuwait and the largest American military action in a quarter century—the United States deployed more than a half million soldiers to the Persian Gulf region. Thereafter

American administrations cut the Cold War force, but not as dramatically as might have been expected. In fact, successive American administrations did not view the end of the Cold War as providing a strategic holiday. From the first Bush administration through the Clinton years, American strategy and force planning continued to be based on the premise that the United States might have to fight and win two wars in different regions of the world almost simultaneously. This two-war standard, though often questioned, was never abandoned by military and civilian leaders who believed the United States did have to be prepared to fight wars on the Korean Peninsula and in the Persian Gulf. The fact that the United States could even consider maintaining such a capability set it far apart from its European allies, who on their own lacked the capacity to fight even one small war close to home, let alone two large wars thousands of miles away. By historical standards, America's post–Cold War military power, particularly its ability to project that power to all corners of the globe, remained unprecedented.

Meanwhile, the very fact of the Soviet empire's collapse vastly increased America's strength relative to the rest of the world. The sizable American military arsenal, once barely sufficient to balance Soviet power, was now deployed in a world without a single formidable adversary. This "unipolar moment" had an entirely natural and predictable consequence: It made the United States more willing to use force abroad. With the check of Soviet power removed, the United States was free to intervene practically wherever and whenever it chose—a fact reflected in the proliferation of overseas military interventions that began during the first Bush administration with the invasion of Panama in 1989, the Persian Gulf War in 1991, and the humanitarian intervention in Somalia in 1992, and continued during the Clinton years with interventions in Haiti, Bosnia, and Kosovo. While many American politicians talked of pulling back from the world, the reality was an America intervening abroad more frequently than it had throughout most of the Cold War. Thanks to the new technologies, the United States was also freer to use force around the world in more limited ways through air and missile strikes, which it did with increasing frequency. The end of the Cold War thus expanded an already wide gulf between European and American power.

PSYCHOLOGIES OF POWER
AND WEAKNESS

How could this great and growing disparity of power fail to create a growing gap in strategic perceptions and strategic "culture"? Strong powers naturally view the world differently than weaker powers. They measure risks and threats differently, they define security differently, and they have different levels of tolerance for insecurity. Those with great military power are more likely to consider force a useful tool of international relations than those who have less military power. The stronger may, in fact, rely on force more than they should. One British critic of America's propensity to military action recalls the old saw "When you have a hammer, all problems start to look like nails." This is true. But nations without great military power face the opposite danger: When you don't have a hammer, you don't want anything to look like a nail. The perspectives and psychologies of power and weakness explain much, though certainly not all, of what divides the United States and Europe today.

The problem is not new. During the Cold War, American military predominance and Europe's relative weakness produced important and sometimes serious disagreements over the U.S.-Soviet arms race and American interventions in the third world. Gaullism, *Ostpolitik*, and the various movements for European independence and unity were manifestations not only of a European desire for honor and freedom of action. They also reflected a European conviction that America's approach to the Cold War was too confrontational, too militaristic, and too dangerous. After the very early years of the Cold War, when Churchill and others sometimes worried that the United States was too gentle in dealing with Stalin, it was usually the Americans who pushed for tougher forms of containment and the Europeans who resisted. The Europeans believed they knew better how to deal with the Soviets: through engagement and seduction, through commercial and political ties, through patience and forbearance. It was a legitimate view, shared at times by many Americans, especially during and after the Vietnam War, when American leaders believed they, too, were working from a position of weakness. But Europeans' repeated dissent from the harder American approach to the Cold War reflected Europe's fundamental and enduring weakness relative to the United States: Europe simply had fewer military options at its disposal, and it was more vulnerable to a powerful

Soviet Union. The European approach may have reflected, too, Europe's memory of continental war. Americans, when they were not themselves engaged in the subtleties of détente, viewed the European approach as a new form of appeasement, a return to the fearful mentality of the 1930s. Europeans viewed it as a policy of sophistication, as a possible escape from what they regarded as Washington's excessively confrontational approach to the Cold War.

During the Cold War, however, these were more tactical than philosophical disagreements. They were not arguments about the purposes of power, since both sides of the Atlantic clearly relied on their pooled military power to deter any possible Soviet attack, no matter how remote the chances of such an attack might seem. The end of the Cold War, which both widened the power gap and removed the common Soviet enemy, not only exacerbated the difference in strategic perspectives but also changed the nature of the argument.

For much of the 1990s, nostalgic policymakers and analysts on both sides of the Atlantic insisted that Americans and Europeans mostly agreed on the nature of these threats to peace and world order; where they disagreed was on the question of how to respond. This sunny analysis overlooked the growing divide. More and more over the past decade, the United States and its European allies have had rather substantial disagreements over what constitute intolerable threats to international security and the world order, as the case of Iraq has abundantly shown. And these disagreements reflect, above all, the disparity of power.

One of the biggest transatlantic disagreements since the end of the Cold War has been over which "new" threats merit the most attention. American administrations have placed the greatest emphasis on so-called rogue states and what President George W. Bush a year ago called the "axis of evil." Most Europeans have taken a calmer view of the risks posed by these regimes. As a French official once told me, "The problem is 'failed states,' not 'rogue states.'"

Why should Americans and Europeans view the same threats differently? Europeans often argue that Americans have an unreasonable demand for "perfect" security, the product of living for centuries shielded behind two oceans.[20] Europeans claim they know what it is like to live with danger, to exist side by side with evil, since they've done it for centuries—hence their greater tolerance for such threats as may be posed by Saddam Hussein's Iraq, the ayatollahs' Iran, or North Korea. Americans, they claim, make far too much of the dangers these regimes pose.

But there is less to this cultural explanation than meets the eye. The United States in its formative decades lived in a state of substantial insecurity, surrounded by hostile European empires on the North American continent, at constant risk of being torn apart by centrifugal forces that were encouraged by threats from without: National insecurity formed the core of George Washington's Farewell Address. As for the Europeans' supposed tolerance for insecurity and evil, it can be overstated. For the better part of three centuries, European Catholics and Protestants

---

[20] For that matter, this is also the view commonly found in American textbooks.

more often preferred to kill than to tolerate each other; nor have the past two centuries shown all that much mutual tolerance between French and Germans. Some Europeans argue that precisely because Europe has suffered so much, it has a higher tolerance for suffering than America and therefore a higher tolerance for threats. More likely the opposite is true. The memory of the First World War made the British and French publics more fearful of Nazi Germany, not more tolerant, and this attitude contributed significantly to the appeasement strategy of the 1930s.

A better explanation of Europe's greater tolerance for threats today is its relative weakness. The differing psychologies of power and weakness are easy enough to understand. A man armed only with a knife may decide that a bear prowling the forest is a tolerable danger, inasmuch as the alternative—hunting the bear armed only with a knife—is actually riskier than lying low and hoping the bear never attacks. The same man armed with a rifle, however, will likely make a different calculation of what constitutes a tolerable risk. Why should he risk being mauled to death if he doesn't have to? This perfectly normal human psychology has driven a wedge between the United States and Europe. The vast majority of Europeans always believed that the threat posed by Saddam Hussein was more tolerable than the risk of removing him. But Americans, being stronger, developed a lower threshold of tolerance for Saddam and his weapons of mass destruction, especially after September 11. Both assessments made sense, given the differing perspectives of a powerful America and a weaker Europe. Europeans like to say that Americans are obsessed with fixing problems, but it is generally true that those with a greater capacity to fix problems are more likely to try to fix them than those who have no such capability. Americans could imagine successfully invading Iraq and toppling Saddam, and therefore by the end of 2002 more than 70 percent of Americans favored such action. Not surprisingly, Europeans found the prospect both unimaginable and frightening.

The incapacity to respond to threats leads not only to tolerance. It can also lead to denial. It is normal to try to put out of one's mind that which one can do nothing about. According to one student of European opinion, even the very focus on "threats" differentiates American policymakers from their European counterparts. Americans, writes Steven Everts, talk about foreign "threats" such as "the proliferation of weapons of mass destruction, terrorism, and 'rogue states.'" But Europeans look at "challenges," such as "ethnic conflict, migration, organized crime, poverty and environmental degradation." As Everts notes, however, the key difference is less a matter of culture and philosophy than of capability. Europeans "are most worried about issues . . . that have a greater chance of being solved by political engagement and huge sums of money."[21] In other words, Europeans focus on issues—"challenges"—where European strengths come into play, but not on those "threats" where European weakness

---

[21] Steven Everts, "Unilateral America, Lightweight Europe?: Managing Divergence in Transatlantic Foreign Policy," working paper, Centre for European Reform, February 2001.

makes solutions elusive. If Europe's strategic culture today places less value on hard power and military strength and more value on such soft-power tools as economics and trade, isn't it partly because Europe is militarily weak and economically strong? Americans are quicker to acknowledge the existence of threats, even to perceive them where others may not see any, because they can conceive of doing something to meet those threats.

The differing threat perceptions in the United States and Europe are not just matters of psychology, however. They are also grounded in a practical reality that is another product of the disparity of power and the structure of the present international order. For while Iraq and other rogue states have posed a threat to Europe, objectively they have *not* posed the same level of threat to Europeans as they have to the United States. There is, first of all, the American security guarantee that Europeans enjoy and have enjoyed for six decades, ever since the United States took upon itself the burden of maintaining order in far-flung regions of the world—from East Asia to the Middle East—from which European power had largely withdrawn. Europeans have generally believed, whether or not they admit it to themselves, that whenever Iraq or some other rogue nation emerged as a real and present danger, as opposed to merely a potential danger, then the United States would do something about it. If during the Cold War Europe by necessity made a major contribution to its own defense, since the end of the Cold War Europeans have enjoyed an unparalleled measure of "free security" because most of the likely threats emanate from regions outside Europe, where only the United States can project effective force. In a very practical sense—that is, when it comes to actual strategic planning—Iraq, North Korea, Iran, or any other rogue state in the world has not been primarily a European problem. Nor, certainly, is China. Both Europeans and Americans agree that these are primarily American problems.

This is why Saddam Hussein was never perceived to be the threat to Europe that he was to the United States. The logical consequence of the transatlantic disparity of power has been that the task of containing Saddam Hussein always belonged primarily to the United States, not to Europe, and everyone agreed on this[22]—including Saddam, which was why he always considered the United States, not Europe, his principal adversary. In the Persian Gulf, the Middle East, and most other regions of the world (including Europe), the United States plays the role of ultimate enforcer. "You are so powerful," Europeans often say to Americans. "So why do you feel so threatened?" But it is precisely America's great power and its willingness to assume the responsibility for protecting other nations that make it the primary target, and often the only target. Most Europeans have been understandably content that it should remain so.

A poll of European and American opinion taken in the summer of 2002 nicely revealed this transatlantic gap in perceptions of threat. Although widely reported as showing American and European publics in rough agreement, the results indicated many more Americans than Euro-

[22] Notwithstanding the sizable British contribution to military operations in Iraq.

peans worried about the threat posed not only by Iraq, Iran, and North Korea, but also by China, Russia, the India-Pakistan confrontation, and even the conflict between Israel and the Arab states—on almost all these issues significantly more Americans than Europeans expressed concern.[23] But why should Americans, "protected by two oceans," be more worried about a conflagration on the Asian subcontinent or in the Middle East or in Russia than the Europeans, who live so much closer? The answer is that Americans know that when international crises erupt, whether in the Taiwan Strait or in Kashmir, they are likely to be the first to become involved. Europeans know this, too. Polls that show Americans worrying more than Europeans about all nature of global security threats and Europeans worrying more about global warming demonstrate that both sets of publics have a remarkably accurate sense of their nations' very different global roles.

Americans are "cowboys," Europeans love to say. And there is truth in this. The United States does act as an international sheriff, self-appointed perhaps but widely

[23] The poll, sponsored by the German Marshall Fund and the Chicago Council on Foreign Relations, was taken between June 1 and July 6, 2002. Asked to identify which "possible threats to vital interests" were "extremely important," 91 percent of Americans listed "international terrorism" as opposed to 65 percent of Europeans. On "Iraq developing weapons of mass destruction," the gap was 28 points, with 86 percent of Americans identifying Iraq as an "extremely important" threat compared to 58 percent of Europeans. On "Islamic fundamentalism," 61–49; on "military conflict between Israel and Arab neighbors," 67–43; on "tensions between India and Pakistan," 54–32; on "development of China as a world power," 56–19; on "political turmoil in Russia," 27–15.

welcomed nevertheless, trying to enforce some peace and justice in what Americans see as a lawless world where outlaws need to be deterred or destroyed, often through the muzzle of a gun. Europe, by this Wild West analogy, is more like the saloonkeeper. Outlaws shoot sheriffs, not saloonkeepers. In fact, from the saloonkeeper's point of view, the sheriff trying to impose order by force can sometimes be more threatening than the outlaws, who, at least for the time being, may just want a drink.

When Europeans took to the streets by the millions after September 11, most Americans believed it was out of a sense of shared danger and common interest: The Europeans knew they could be next. But Europeans by and large did not feel that way. Europeans have never really believed they are next. They could be secondary targets—because they are allied with the United States—but they are not the primary target, because they no longer play the imperial role in the Middle East that might have engendered the same antagonism against them as is aimed at the United States. When Europeans wept and waved American flags after September 11, it was out of genuine human sympathy. It was an expression of sorrow and affection for Americans. For better or for worse, European displays of solidarity were a product more of fellow feeling than of careful calculations of self-interest. Europeans' heartfelt sympathy, unaccompanied by a sense of shared risk and common responsibility, did not draw Europeans and Americans together in strategic partnership. On the contrary, as soon as Americans began looking beyond the immediate task of finding and destroying

Osama bin Laden and Al Qaeda to broader strategic goals in the "war on terrorism," Europeans recoiled.

Differing perceptions of threats and how to address them are in some ways only the surface manifestation of more fundamental differences in the worldviews of a strong United States and a relatively weaker Europe. It is not just that Europeans and Americans have not shared the same view of what to do about a specific problem such as Iraq. They do not share the same broad view of how the world should be governed, about the role of international institutions and international law, about the proper balance between the use of force and the use of diplomacy in international affairs.

Some of this difference is related to the power gap. Europe's relative weakness has understandably produced a powerful European interest in building a world where military strength and hard power matter less than economic and soft power, an international order where international law and international institutions matter more than the power of individual nations, where unilateral action by powerful states is forbidden, where all nations regardless of their strength have equal rights and are equally protected by commonly agreed-upon international rules of behavior. Because they are relatively weak, Europeans have a deep interest in devaluing and eventually eradicating the brutal laws of an anarchic Hobbesian world where power is the ultimate determinant of national security and success.

This is no reproach. It is what weaker powers have wanted from time immemorial. It was what Americans wanted in the eighteenth and early nineteenth centuries, when the brutality of a European system of power politics run by the global giants of France, Britain, and Russia left Americans constantly vulnerable to imperial thrashing. It was what the other small powers of Europe wanted in those years, too, only to be sneered at by Bourbon kings and other powerful monarchs, who spoke instead of *raison d'état*. The great proponent of international law on the high seas in the eighteenth century was the United States; the great opponent was Britain's navy, the "mistress of the seas." In an anarchic world, small powers always fear they will be victims. Great powers, on the other hand, often fear rules that may constrain them more than they do anarchy. In an anarchic world, they rely on their power to provide security and prosperity.

This natural and historic disagreement between the stronger and the weaker manifests itself in today's transatlantic dispute over the issue of unilateralism. Europeans generally believe their objection to American unilateralism is proof of their greater commitment to principles of world order. And it is true that their commitment to those ideals, although not absolute, is greater than that of most Americans. But Europeans are less willing to acknowledge another truth: that their hostility to unilateralism is also self-interested. Since Europeans lack the capacity to undertake unilateral military actions, either individually or collectively as "Europe," it is natural that they should oppose allowing others to do what they cannot do themselves. For Europeans, the appeal to multilateralism and international law has a real practical payoff and little cost.

The same cannot be said of the United States. Polls

consistently show that Americans support multilateral action in principle. They even support acting under the rubric of the United Nations, which, after all, Americans created. But the fact remains that the United States can act unilaterally and has done so many times with reasonable success. The facile assertion that the United States cannot "go it alone" is more a hopeful platitude than a description of reality. Americans certainly prefer to act together with others, and American actions stand a better chance of success if the United States has allies. But if it were literally true that the United States could not act unilaterally, we wouldn't be having a grand transatlantic debate over American unilateralism. The problem today, if it is a problem, is that the United States *can* "go it alone," and it is hardly surprising that the American superpower should wish to preserve its ability to do so. Geopolitical logic dictates that Americans have a less compelling interest than Europeans in upholding multilateralism as a universal principle for governing the behavior of nations. Whether unilateral action is a good or a bad thing, Americans objectively have more to lose from outlawing it than any other power in today's unipolar world. Indeed, for Americans to share the European perspective on the virtues of multilateralism, they would have to be even more devoted to the ideals and principles of an international legal order than Europeans are. For Europeans, ideals and interests converge in a world governed according to the principle of multilateralism. For Americans, they do not converge as much.

It is also understandable that Europeans should fear American unilateralism and seek to constrain it as best they can through such institutions as the United Nations. Those who cannot act unilaterally themselves naturally want to have a mechanism for controlling those who can. From the European perspective, the United States may be a relatively benign hegemon, but insofar as its actions delay the arrival of a world order more conducive to the safety of weaker powers, it is objectively dangerous. This is one reason why in recent years a principal objective of European foreign policy has become, as one European observer puts it, the "multilateralising" of the United States.[24] It is why Europeans insist that the United States act only with the approval of the UN Security Council. The Security Council is a pale approximation of a genuine multilateral order, for it was designed by the United States to give the five "great powers" of the postwar era an exclusive authority to decide what was and was not legitimate international action. Today the Security Council contains only one "great power," the United States. But the Security Council is nevertheless the one place where a weaker nation such as France has at least the theoretical power to control American actions, *if* the United States can be persuaded to come to the Security Council and be bound by its decisions. For Europeans, the UN Security Council is a substitute for the power they lack.

Indeed, despite the predictions of Huntington and many realist theorists, the Europeans have not sought to check the rising power of the American colossus by amassing a countervailing power of their own. Clearly

[24] Everts, "Unilateral America, Lightweight Europe?"

they do not consider even a unilateralist United States a sufficient threat to make them increase defense spending to contain it. Nor are they willing to risk their vast trade with the United States by attempting to wield their economic power against the hegemon. Nor are they willing to ally themselves with China, which is willing to spend money on defense, in order to counterbalance the United States. Instead, Europeans hope to contain American power without wielding power themselves. In what may be the ultimate feat of subtlety and indirection, they want to control the behemoth by appealing to its conscience.

It is a sound strategy, as far as it goes. The United States *is* a behemoth with a conscience. It is not Louis XIV's France or George III's England. Americans do not argue, even to themselves, that their actions may be justified by *raison d'état*. They do not claim the right of the stronger or insist to the rest of the world, as the Athenians did at Melos, that "the strong rule where they can and the weak suffer what they must." Americans have never accepted the principles of Europe's old order nor embraced the Machiavellian perspective. The United States is a liberal, progressive society through and through, and to the extent that Americans believe in power, they believe it must be a means of advancing the principles of a liberal civilization and a liberal world order. Americans even share Europe's aspirations for a more orderly world system based not on power but on rules—after all, they were striving for such a world when Europeans were still extolling the laws of *Machtpolitik*. But while these common ideals and aspirations shape foreign policies on both sides of the Atlantic, they cannot completely negate the very different perspectives from which Europeans and Americans view the world and the role of power in international affairs.

HYPERPUISSANCE

The present transatlantic tensions did not begin with the inauguration of George W. Bush in January 2001, nor did they begin after September 11. While the ham-handed diplomacy of the Bush administration in its early months certainly drew a sharper line under the differing European and American perspectives on the issues of international governance, and while the attacks of September 11 shone the brightest possible light on the transatlantic gulf in strategic perceptions, those divisions were already evident during the Clinton years and even during the first Bush administration. As early as 1992, mutual recriminations had been rife over Bosnia. The first Bush administration refused to act, believing it had more important strategic obligations elsewhere. Europeans declared they would act—it was, they insisted, "the hour of Europe"—but the declaration proved hollow when it became clear that Europe could not act even in Bosnia without the United States. When France and Germany took the first small steps to create something like an independent European defense force, the Bush administration scowled. From the European point of view, it was the worst of both worlds. The United States was losing interest in preserving European security, but at the same time it was hostile to European aspirations to take on the task themselves.[25] Europeans complained about American perfidy, and Americans complained about European weakness and ingratitude.

Today many Europeans view the Clinton years as a time of transatlantic harmony, but it was during those years that Europeans began complaining about American power and arrogance in the post–Cold War world. It was during the Clinton years that then–French foreign minister Hubert Védrine coined the term *hyperpuissance* to describe an American behemoth too worryingly powerful to be designated merely a superpower. And it was during the 1990s that Europeans began to view the United States as a "hectoring hegemon." Such complaints were directed especially at Secretary of State Madeleine Albright, whom one American critic described, a bit hyperbolically, as "the first Secretary of State in American history whose diplomatic specialty . . . is lecturing other governments, using threatening language and tastelessly bragging of the power and virtue of her country."[26]

Even in the 1990s the issue on which American and European policies began most notably to diverge was Iraq. Europeans were appalled when Albright and other administration officials in 1997 began suggesting that the eco-

[25] Charles Grant, "European Defence Post-Kosovo?," working paper, Centre for European Reform, June 1999, p. 2.

[26] The comment was by former State Department adviser Charles Maechling Jr., quoted in Thomas W. Lippman, *Madeleine Albright and the New American Diplomacy* (Boulder, CO, 2000), p. 165.

nomic sanctions placed on Iraq after the Gulf War could not be lifted while Saddam Hussein remained in power. They believed, in classically European fashion, that Iraq should be offered incentives for better behavior, not threatened, in classically American fashion, with more economic or military coercion. The growing split between the United States and its allies on the Iraq question came into the open at the end of 1997, when the Clinton administration tried to increase the pressure on Baghdad to cooperate with UN arms inspectors, and France joined Russia and China in blocking the American proposals in the UN Security Council. When the Clinton administration finally turned to the use of military force and bombed Iraq in December 1998, it did so without a UN Security Council authorization and with only Great Britain by its side. In its waning months, the Clinton administration continued to believe that "Iraq, under Saddam Hussein, remains dangerous, unreconstructed, defiant, and isolated." It would "never be able to be rehabilitated or reintegrated into the community of nations" with Saddam in power.[27] This was not the view of France or most of the rest of Europe. The rehabilitation and reintegration of Saddam Hussein's Iraq were precisely what they sought.

It was during the 1990s, too, that some of the contentious issues that would produce transatlantic storms during the second Bush administration made their first appearance. Clinton took the first steps toward construct-

[27] Address by Assistant Secretary of State Martin Indyk to the Council on Foreign Relations, April 22, 1999, quoted in ibid., p. 183.

ing a new missile defense system designed to protect the United States from nuclear-armed rogue states such as North Korea. Such a system threatened to undo the Antiballistic Missile Treaty and the doctrine of mutually assured destruction that Europeans had long valued as central to their own strategic security. It also threatened to protect American soil while leaving Europeans still vulnerable to nuclear attack, which Europeans understandably considered undesirable. The Clinton administration negotiated the Kyoto protocol to address global climate change but deliberately did not submit it to the Senate, where it was certain to be defeated. And it was the Clinton administration, prodded by Secretary of Defense William Cohen and senior military officials at the Pentagon, that first demanded that American troops be immune from prosecution by the new International Criminal Court—which had become the quintessential symbol of European aspirations to a world in which all nations were equal under the law. In taking this tack away from the European multilateralist consensus, President Clinton was to some extent bowing to pressures from a hostile Republican-dominated Congress. But the Clinton administration itself believed those treaties were flawed; even Clinton was not as "European" as he would later be depicted. In any case, the growing divergence between American and European policies during the Clinton years reflected a deeper reality. The United States in the post–Cold War era was becoming more unilateral in its approach to the rest of the world at a time when Europeans were embarking on a new and vigorous effort to build a more comprehensive international legal system precisely to restrain such unilateralism.

The war in Kosovo in the spring of 1999 gave an interesting hint of the future. Although the allied military campaign against Serbia's Slobodan Milosevic was a success, and represented the first occasion in its fifty-year history that NATO had ever undertaken military action, the conflict also revealed subtle fissures in the post–Cold War alliance—fissures that survived Kosovo but might not withstand the greater pressures of a different kind of war under different international circumstances.

The conduct of the war reflected the severe transatlantic military imbalance. The United States flew the majority of missions, almost all of the precision-guided munitions dropped in Serbia and Kosovo were made in America, and the unmatched superiority of American technical intelligence-gathering capabilities meant that 99 percent of the proposed targets came from American intelligence sources. The American dominance of the war effort troubled Europeans in two ways. On the one hand, it was a rather shocking blow to European honor. As two British analysts observed after the war, even the United Kingdom, "which prides itself on being a serious military power, could contribute only 4 per cent of the aircraft and 4 per cent of the bombs dropped."[28] To Europe's most respected strategic thinkers in France, Germany, and Britain, the Kosovo war had only "highlighted the impotence of Europe's armed forces." It was embarrassing

[28] Tim Garden and John Roper, "Pooling Forces," Centre for European Reform, December 1999.

that even in a region as close as the Balkans, Europe's "ability to deploy force" was but "a meager fraction" of America's.[29]

More troubling still was that European dependence on American military power gave the United States dominant influence not only over the way the war was fought but also over international diplomacy before, during, and after the war. Europeans had favored a pause in the bombing after a few days, for instance, to give Milosevic a chance to end the crisis. But the United States and the American NATO commander, General Wesley K. Clark, refused. Most Europeans, especially the French, wanted to escalate the bombing campaign gradually, to reduce the damage to Serbia and give Milosevic incentive to end the conflict before NATO destroyed everything he valued. But Clark disagreed. "In U.S. military thinking," he explains, "we seek to be as decisive as possible once we begin to use force."[30] Many Europeans wanted to focus the bombing on Serbian forces engaged in "ethnic cleansing" in Kosovo. But as Clark recalls, "Most Americans believed that the best and most rapid way to change Milosevic's views was to strike at him and his regime as hard as possible."[31]

Whether the Americans or the Europeans were right about the way that war or any war should be fought, for Europe the depressing fact remained that because the

[29] Christoph Bertram, Charles Grant, and François Heisbourg, "European Defence: The Next Steps," Centre for European Reform, *CER Bulletin* 14 (October/November 2000).

[30] Wesley K. Clark, *Waging Modern War* (New York, 2001), p. 449.

[31] Americans also didn't want their pilots flying at low altitudes where they were more likely to be shot down. Ibid.

Kosovo war was fought with "American equipment," it was fought largely according to "American doctrine."[32] For all Europe's great economic power and for all its success at achieving political union, Europe's military weakness had produced diplomatic weakness and sharply diminished its political influence compared to that of the United States, even in a crisis in Europe.

The Americans were unhappy, too. General Clark and his colleagues complained that the laborious effort to preserve consensus within the alliance hampered the fighting of the war and delayed its successful conclusion. Before the war, Clark later insisted, "we could not present an unambiguous and clear warning to Milosevic," partly because many European countries would not threaten action without a mandate from the UN Security Council—what Clark, in typically American fashion, called Europe's "legal issues." For the Americans, these "legal issues" were "obstacles to properly planning and preparing" for the war.[33] During the fighting, Clark and his American colleagues were exasperated by the need constantly to find compromise between American military doctrine and what Clark called the "European approach."[34] "It was always the Americans who pushed for the escalation to new, more sensitive targets . . . and always some of the Allies who expressed doubts and reservations." In

---

[32] Garden and Roper, "Pooling Forces."

[33] Clark, *Waging Modern War*, pp. 420, 421. "The lack of legal authority," Clark recalls, "caused almost every NATO government initially to reject Secretary Cohen's appeal to authorize a NATO threat" prior to the outbreak of war in early 1999.

[34] Ibid., p. 449.

Clark's view, "We paid a price in operational effectiveness by having to constrain the nature of the operation to fit within the political and legal concerns of NATO member nations."[35] The result was a war that neither Europeans nor Americans liked. In a meeting of NATO defense ministers a few months after the war, one minister remarked that the biggest lesson of the allied war in Kosovo was that "we never want to do this again."[36]

Fortunately for the health of the alliance in 1999, Clark and his superiors in the Clinton administration believed the price for allied unity was worth paying. But American willingness to preserve transatlantic cohesion even at the cost of military effectiveness owed a great deal to the special, if not unique, circumstances of the Kosovo conflict. For the United States, preserving the cohesion and viability of the alliance was not just a means to an end in Kosovo; it was among the primary aims of the American intervention, just as saving the alliance had been a primary motive for America's earlier intervention in Bosnia, and just as preserving the cohesion of the alliance had been a primary goal of American strategy during the Cold War.

American abstention from the Balkan conflict during the first Bush administration and in Clinton's first term had seemed to threaten NATO itself. When Secretary of State James Baker referred to the Balkan war as a strictly "European conflict" and declared that the United States did not have "a dog in that fight," such sentiments, widely

35 Ibid., p. 426.
36 As Clark wryly reports, "No one laughed." Ibid., p. 417.

shared among his colleagues, including especially then–Chairman of the Joint Chiefs of Staff Colin Powell, had raised troubling questions about America's role in Europe in the post–Cold War world. Was the United States still committed to European security and stability? Could NATO meet what were then considered to be the new challenges of the post–Cold War era, ethnic conflict and the collapse of states? Or had the American-led alliance outlived its usefulness to the point where it could not stop aggression and ethnic cleansing even on the European continent?

American involvement in Kosovo or Bosnia was not based on calculations of a narrow American "national interest," at least as most Americans understood the term. While Americans had a compelling moral interest in stopping genocide and ethnic cleansing, especially in Europe, American realist theorists insisted the United States had no "national interest" at stake in the Balkans. When Clinton officials and other supporters of American intervention defended American military action on the grounds of the national interest, it was as a means of preserving the alliance and repairing the frayed bonds of the trans-atlantic relationship. As in the Cold War, America fought in the Balkans ultimately to preserve "the West." And that goal determined American military strategy. As General Clark puts it, "No single target or set of targets was more important than NATO cohesion."[37]

Such an approach to fighting the war may have been sound in Kosovo and Bosnia. But it raised questions about

[37] Ibid., p. 430.

the future. Would Clark or any future American commander make the same calculation in different circumstances? Would he be willing to sacrifice operational effectiveness, rapid escalation, "American military doctrine," and the use of decisive force in a war whose primary goal was not the cohesion and preservation of NATO and Europe? In fact, the Kosovo war showed how difficult it was going to be for the United States and its European allies to fight any war together. What if they had to fight a war not primarily "humanitarian" in nature? What if Americans believed their vital interests were directly threatened? What if Americans had suffered horrendous attacks on their own territory and feared more attacks were coming? Would Americans in such circumstances have the same tolerance for the clumsy and constrained NATO decision-making and war-fighting process? Would they want to compromise again with the "European approach" to warfare, or would they prefer to "go it alone"? The answer to those questions came after September 11. With almost three thousand dead in New York City, and Osama bin Laden on the loose in Afghanistan, the U.S. military and the Bush administration had little interest in working through NATO. This may have been unfortunate from the perspective of transatlantic relations, but it was hardly surprising.

The fact is that by the end of the 1990s the disparity of power was subtly rending the fabric of the transatlantic relationship. The Americans were unhappy and impatient about constraints imposed by European allies who brought so little to a war but whose concern for "legal issues" prevented the war's effective prosecution. The

Europeans were unhappy about American dominance and their own dependence. The lesson for Americans, including the top officials in the Clinton administration, was that even with the best intentions, multilateral action could not succeed without a significant element of American unilateralism, an American willingness to use its overwhelming power to dominate both war and diplomacy when weaker allies hesitated. The Clinton administration had come into office talking about "assertive multilateralism"; it ended up talking about America as "the indispensable nation."

The lesson for many Europeans was that Europe needed to take steps to release itself at least partially from a dependence on American power that, after the Cold War, seemed no longer necessary. This, in turn, required that Europe create some independent military capability. At the end of 1998, that judgment prompted no less a friend of the United States than Tony Blair to reach across the Channel to France with an unprecedented offer to add Britain's weight to hitherto stalled efforts to create a common European Union defense capability independent of NATO. Together, Blair and Jacques Chirac won Europewide approval for building a force of 60,000 troops that could be deployed far from home and sustained for up to a year.

Once again, had this Anglo-French initiative borne fruit, the United States and Europe might today be in the process of establishing a new relationship based on a greater European military capability and greater independence from American power. But this initiative is headed the way of all other proposals to enhance European military power and strategic self-reliance. In December 2001 the Belgian foreign minister suggested that the EU military force should simply "declare itself operational without such a declaration being based on any true capability."[38] In fact, the effort to build a European force has so far been an embarrassment to Europeans. Today, the European Union is no closer to fielding an independent force, even a small one, than it was three years ago. And this latest failure raises the question that so many Europeans and so many "transatlanticists" in the United States have been unwilling even to ask, much less to answer: Why hasn't Europe fulfilled the promise of the European Union in foreign and defense policy, or met the promptings of some of its most important leaders to build up even enough military power to tilt the balance, just a little, away from American dominance?

THE POSTMODERN PARADISE

The answer lies somewhere in the realm of ideology, in European attitudes not just toward defense spending but toward power itself. Important as the power gap has been in shaping the respective strategic cultures of the United States and Europe, if the disparity of military capabilities were the only problem, the solution would be fairly straightforward. With a highly educated and productive population of almost 400 million people and a $9 trillion economy, Europe today has the wealth and technological

[38] John Vinocur, "On Both War and Peace, the EU Stands Divided," *International Herald Tribune*, December 17, 2001.

capability to make itself more of a world power in military terms if Europeans wanted to become that kind of world power. They could easily spend twice as much as they are currently spending on defense if they believed it necessary to do so.[39] And closing the power gap between the United States and Europe would probably go some way toward closing the gap in strategic perceptions.

There is a cynical view current in American strategic circles that the Europeans simply enjoy the "free ride" they have gotten under the American security umbrella over the past six decades. Given America's willingness to spend so much money protecting them, Europeans would rather spend their own money on social welfare programs, long vacations, and shorter workweeks. But there is more to the transatlantic gulf than a gap in military capabilities, and while Europe may be enjoying a free ride in terms of global security, there is more to Europe's unwillingness to build up its military power than comfort with the present American guarantee. After all, the United States in the nineteenth century was the beneficiary of the British navy's dominance of the Atlantic and the Caribbean. But that did not stop the United States from engaging in its own peacetime naval buildup in the 1880s and 1890s, a buildup that equipped it to launch and win the Spanish-

---

[39] Europeans insist that there are certain structural realities in their national budgets, built-in limitations to any significant increases in defense spending. But if Europe were about to be invaded, would its politicians insist that defense budgets could not be raised because this would violate the terms of the EU's growth and stability pact? If Germans truly felt threatened, would they insist nevertheless that their social welfare programs be left untouched?

American War, acquire the Philippines, and become a world power. Late-nineteenth-century Americans did not take comfort from their security; they were ambitious for more power.

Europeans today are not ambitious for power, and certainly not for military power. Europeans over the past half century have developed a genuinely different perspective on the role of power in international relations, a perspective that springs directly from their unique historical experience since the end of World War II. They have rejected the power politics that brought them such misery over the past century and more. This is a perspective on power that Americans do not and cannot share, inasmuch as the formative historical experiences on their side of the Atlantic have not been the same.

Consider again the qualities that make up the European strategic culture: the emphasis on negotiation, diplomacy, and commercial ties, on international law over the use of force, on seduction over coercion, on multilateralism over unilateralism. It is true that these are not traditionally European approaches to international relations when viewed from a long historical perspective. But they are a product of more recent European history. The modern European strategic culture represents a conscious rejection of the European past, a rejection of the evils of European *Machtpolitik*. It is a reflection of Europeans' ardent and understandable desire never to return to that past. Who knows better than Europeans the dangers that arise from unbridled power politics, from an excessive reliance on military force, from policies produced by national egoism and ambition, even from balance of power and *raison d'état*? As German Foreign Minister Joschka Fischer put it in a speech outlining his vision of the European future, "The core of the concept of Europe after 1945 was and still is a rejection of the European balance-of-power principle and the hegemonic ambitions of individual states that had emerged following the Peace of Westphalia in 1648."[40] The European Union is itself the product of an awful century of European warfare.

Of course, it was the "hegemonic ambitions" of one nation in particular that European integration was meant to contain. And it is the integration and taming of Germany that is the great accomplishment of Europe—viewed historically, perhaps the greatest feat of international politics ever achieved. Some Europeans recall, as Fischer does, the central role the United States played in solving the "German problem." Fewer like to recall that the military destruction of Nazi Germany was the prerequisite for the European peace that followed. Instead, most Europeans like to believe that it was the transformation of the European mind and spirit that made possible the "new order." The Europeans, who invented power politics, turned themselves into born-again idealists by an act of will, leaving behind them what Fischer called "the old system of balance with its continued national orientation, constraints of coalition, traditional interest-led politics and the permanent danger of nationalist ideologies and confrontations."

Fischer stands near one end of the spectrum of European idealism. But this is not really a right-left issue in Europe. Fischer's principal contention—that Europe has

[40] Fischer speech at Humboldt University in Berlin, May 12, 2000.

moved beyond the old system of power politics and discovered a new system for preserving peace in international
relations—is widely shared across Europe. As senior British
diplomat and EU official Robert Cooper has argued,
Europe today lives in a "postmodern system" that does not
rest on a balance of power but on "the rejection of force"
and on "self-enforced rules of behavior." In the "postmodern world," writes Cooper, "*raison d'état* and the amorality
of Machiavelli's theories of statecraft . . . have been replaced
by a moral consciousness" in international affairs.[41]

American realists might scoff at this idealism. Hans
Morgenthau and George Kennan assumed that only naïve
Americans succumbed to such "Wilsonian" legalistic and
moralistic fancies, not those war-tested, historically minded
European Machiavels. But, really, why shouldn't Europeans be idealistic about international affairs, at least
as they are conducted in Europe's "postmodern system"?
Within the confines of Europe, the age-old laws of international relations have been repealed. Europeans have
pursued their new order, freed from the laws and even the
mentality of power politics. Europeans have stepped out
of the Hobbesian world of anarchy into the Kantian world
of perpetual peace.

In fact, the United States solved the Kantian paradox
for the Europeans. Kant had argued that the only solution
to the immoral horrors of the Hobbesian world was the
creation of a world government. But he also feared that
the "state of universal peace" made possible by world government would be an even greater threat to human free-

[41] Robert Cooper, *The Observer*, April 7, 2002.

dom than the Hobbesian international order, inasmuch as such a government, with its monopoly of power, would become "the most horrible despotism."[42] How nations could achieve perpetual peace without destroying human freedom was a problem Kant could not solve. But for Europe the problem was solved by the United States. By providing security from outside, the United States rendered it unnecessary for Europe's supranational government to provide it. Europeans did not need power to achieve peace, and they do not need power to preserve it.

European life during the more than five decades since the end of World War II has been shaped not by the brutal laws of power politics but by the unfolding of a geopolitical fantasy, a miracle of world-historical importance: The German lion has lain down with the French lamb. The conflict that ravaged Europe ever since the violent birth of Germany in the nineteenth century has been put to rest. The means by which this miracle has been achieved have understandably acquired something of a sacred mystique for Europeans, especially since the end of the Cold War. Diplomacy, negotiations, patience, the forging of economic ties, political engagement, the use of inducements rather than sanctions, compromise rather than confrontation, the taking of small steps and tempering ambitions for success—these were the tools of Franco-German rapprochement and hence the tools that made European integration possible. France, in particular, took the leap into the unknown, offering to pool first economic and

[42] See Thomas L. Pangle and Peter J. Ahrensdorf, *Justice Among Nations: On the Moral Basis of Power and Peace* (Lawrence, KS, 1999), pp. 200–201.

then political sovereignty with its old German enemy as the best means of preventing future conflicts. Germany, in turn, ceded its own great power within Europe in the interest of reintegration.

The integration of Europe was not to be based on military deterrence or the balance of power. To the contrary, the miracle came from the rejection of military power and of its utility as an instrument of international affairs—at least within the confines of Europe. During the Cold War, few Europeans doubted the need for military power to deter the Soviet Union. But the end of the Cold War, by removing even the external danger of the Soviet Union, allowed Europe's new order, and its new idealism, to blossom fully into a grand plan for world order. Freed from the requirements of any military deterrence, internal or external, Europeans became still more confident that their way of settling international problems now had universal application. Their belief in the importance and relevance of security organizations like NATO diminished by equal measure.

"The genius of the founding fathers," European Commission President Romano Prodi explained, "lay in translating extremely high political ambitions . . . into a series of more specific, almost technical decisions. This indirect approach made further action possible. Rapprochement took place gradually. From confrontation we moved to willingness to cooperate in the economic sphere and then on to integration."[43] This is what many Europeans

[43] Speech by Romano Prodi at the Institut d'Etudes Politiques in Paris, May 29, 2001.

believe they have to offer the world: not power, but the transcendence of power. The "essence" of the European Union, writes Everts, is "all about subjecting inter-state relations to the rule of law," and Europe's experience of successful multilateral governance has, in turn, produced an ambition to convert the world.[44] Europe "has a role to play in world 'governance,' " says Prodi, a role based on replicating the European experience on a global scale. In Europe "the rule of law has replaced the crude interplay of power . . . power politics have lost their influence." And by "making a success of integration we are demonstrating to the world that it is possible to create a method for peace."

No doubt there are Britons, Germans, French, and others who would frown on such exuberant idealism. But many Europeans, including many in positions of power, routinely apply Europe's experience to the rest of the world, and sometimes with the evangelic zeal of converts. The general European critique of the American approach to rogue regimes is based on this special European insight. Iraq, North Korea, Iran, Libya—these states may be dangerous and unpleasant, and even, if simplistic Americans insist, evil. But Germany was evil once, too. Might not an "indirect approach" work again, as it did in Europe? Might it not be possible once more to move from confrontation to rapprochement, beginning with cooperation in the economic sphere and then moving on to peaceful integration? Could not the formula that worked in Europe work again with Iran? Might it have even worked with Iraq? A great many Europeans have insisted that it might, and at less

[44] Everts, "Unilateral America, Lightweight Europe?," p. 10.

cost and risk than war. And Europe would apply its lesson to Israelis and Palestinians as well, for, after all, as EU Commissioner Chris Patten argues, "European integration shows that compromise and reconciliation is possible after generations of prejudice, war and suffering."[45] The transmission of the European miracle to the rest of the world has become Europe's new *mission civilisatrice.* Just as Americans have always believed that they had discovered the secret to human happiness and wished to export it to the rest of the world, so Europeans have a new mission born of their own discovery of perpetual peace.

Thus we arrive at what may be the most important reason for the divergence in views between Europe and the United States. America's power and its willingness to exercise that power—unilaterally if necessary—constitute a threat to Europe's new sense of mission. Perhaps it is the greatest threat. American policymakers have found it hard to believe, but leading officials and politicians in Europe really have worried more about how the United States might handle or mishandle the problem of Iraq—by undertaking unilateral and extralegal military action— than they have ever worried about Iraq itself and Saddam Hussein's weapons of mass destruction. And while it is true that they have feared such action might destabilize the Middle East and lead to the unnecessary loss of life, there has always been a deeper concern.[46] Such American

[45] Chris Patten, "From Europe with Support," *Yediot Ahronot,* October 28, 2002.

[46] The common American argument that European policy toward Iraq and Iran has been dictated by financial considerations is only partly right. Are Europeans greedier than Americans? Do American

action, even if successful, is an assault on the essence of "postmodern" Europe. It is an assault on Europe's new ideals, a denial of their universal validity, much as the monarchies of eighteenth- and nineteenth-century Europe were an assault on American republican ideals. Americans ought to be the first to understand that a threat to one's beliefs can be as frightening as a threat to one's physical security.

As Americans have for two centuries, Europeans speak with great confidence of the superiority of their global understanding, the wisdom they have to offer other nations about conflict resolution, and their way of addressing international problems. But just as in the first decade of the American republic, there is a hint of insecurity in the European claim to success, an evident need to have their success affirmed and their views accepted by other nations, particularly by the United States. After all, to deny the validity of the new European idealism is to raise profound doubts about the viability of the European project. If international problems cannot, in fact, be settled the European way, wouldn't that suggest that Europe itself may eventually fall short of a solution, with all the horrors this implies? That is one reason Europeans were so adamant about preserving the universal applicability of the International Criminal Court. For the United States to demand immunity, a double standard for the powerful, is to under-

corporations not influence American policy in Asia and Latin America as well as in the Middle East? The difference is that American strategic judgments sometimes conflict with and override financial interests. For the reasons suggested in this essay, that conflict is much less common for Europeans.

mine the very principle Europeans are trying to establish—
that all nations, strong and weak, are equal under the law
and all must abide by the law. If this principle can be
flouted, even by the benevolent superpower, then what
happens to the European Union, which depends for its very
existence on common obedience to the laws of Europe?
If international law does not reign supreme, is Europe
doomed to return to its past?

And, of course, it is precisely this fear of sliding backward that still hangs over Europeans, even as Europe
moves forward. Europeans, particularly the French and
the Germans, are not entirely sure that the problem once
known as the "German problem" really has been solved.
Neither France under François Mitterrand nor Britain
under Margaret Thatcher was pleased at the prospect of
German reunification after the end of the Cold War; each
had to be coaxed along and reassured by the Americans,
just as British and French leaders had been coaxed along
to accept German reintegration four decades before. As
their various and often very different proposals for the
future constitution of Europe suggest, the French are
still not confident they can trust the Germans, and the
Germans are still not sure they can trust themselves.
Nearly six decades after the end of World War II, a French
official can still remark: "People say, 'It is a terrible thing
that Germany is not working.' But I say, 'Really? When
Germany is working, six months later it is usually march-
ing down the Champs Elysées.' "[47] Buried not very deeply

[47] See Gerard Baker, "Europe's Three Ways of Dealing with Iraq,"
Financial Times, October 17, 2002, p. 17.

beneath the surface of such jokes lies a genuine, lingering trepidation about a Germany that is still too big for the European continent. Last summer, when German Chancellor Gerhard Schroeder defied the Bush administration's call for European support in Iraq, his insistence on dealing with such matters in "the German way" was perhaps even more unsettling to his European neighbors than it was to the United States. Ironically, even German pacifism and neutralism can frighten Europeans when a German leader speaks of "the German way."

Such fears can at times hinder progress toward deeper integration, but they also have driven the European project forward despite innumerable obstacles. European integration is propelled forward in part by the Germans' fears about themselves. The European project must succeed, Joschka Fischer warns, for how else can "the risks and temptations objectively inherent in Germany's dimensions and central situation" be overcome?[48] Those historic German "temptations" play at the back of many a European mind. And every time Europe contemplates the use of military force, or is forced to do so by the United States, there is no avoiding at least momentary consideration of what effect such a military action might have on the "German question" that seems never entirely to disappear.

Perhaps it is not just coincidence, therefore, that the amazing progress toward European integration in recent years has been accompanied not by the emergence of a European superpower but by a diminishing of European

[48] Fischer speech at Humboldt University, May 12, 2000.

military capabilities relative to the United States. Turning Europe into a global superpower capable of balancing the power of the United States may have been one of the original selling points of the European Union—an independent European foreign and defense policy was supposed to be one of the most important by-products of European integration. But, in truth, isn't the ambition for European "power" something of an anachronism? It is an atavistic impulse, inconsistent with the ideals of post-modern Europe, whose very existence depends on the rejection of power politics. Whatever its architects may have intended, European integration has proved to be the enemy of European military power and, indeed, of an important European global role.

This phenomenon has manifested itself not only in flat or declining European defense budgets, but in other ways, too, even in the realm of "soft" power. European leaders talk of Europe's essential role in the world. Prodi yearns "to make our voice heard, to make our actions count."[49] And it is true that Europeans spend a great deal of money on foreign aid—more per capita, they like to point out, than does the United States. Europeans engage in overseas military missions, so long as the missions are mostly limited to peacekeeping. But while the EU periodically dips its fingers into troubled international waters in the Middle East or the Korean Peninsula, the truth is that EU foreign policy is probably the most anemic of all the products of European integration. As one sympathetic observer has noted, few European leaders "are giving it much time or

[49] Prodi speech at the Institut d'Etudes Politiques, May 29, 2001.

energy."[50] EU foreign policy initiatives tend to be short-lived and are rarely backed by sustained agreement on the part of the various European powers. That is one reason they are so easily rebuffed. In the Middle East, where so much European money goes to fund Palestinian and other Arab projects, it is still to the United States that Arabs and Israelis alike look for support, assistance, and a safe resolution of their conflict, not to Europe. All of Europe's great economic power seems not to translate into diplomatic influence, in the Middle East or anywhere else where crises have a military component.[51]

It is obvious, moreover, that issues outside of Europe don't attract nearly as much interest among Europeans as purely European issues do. This has surprised and frustrated Americans on all sides of the political and strategic debate: Recall the profound disappointment of American liberals when Europeans failed to mount an effective protest against Bush's withdrawal from the ABM Treaty. Nor did most Europeans, either among the elites or among the common voters, give the slightest thought to Iraq before the Bush administration threatened to invade it.

This European tendency to look inward is understandable, however, given the enormous and difficult agenda of integration. The enlargement of the European Union to more than two dozen member states, the revision of the common economic and agricultural policies, the question of national sovereignty versus supranational governance,

[50] Charles Grant, "A European View of ESDP," working paper, Centre for European Policy Studies, April 2001.

[51] As Grant observes, "An EU that was less impotent militarily would have more diplomatic clout." Grant, "European Defence," p. 2.

the so-called democracy deficit, the jostling of the large European powers, the dissatisfaction of the smaller powers, the establishment of a new European constitution—all of these present serious and unavoidable challenges. The difficulties of moving forward might seem insuperable were it not for the progress the project of European integration has already demonstrated.

American policies that have been unwelcome in substance—on a missile defense system and the ABM Treaty, belligerence toward Iraq, support for Israel—have been all the more unwelcome because for Europe they are a distraction from the questions that really concern them, namely, questions about Europe. Europeans often point to American insularity and parochialism, but Europeans themselves have turned intensely introspective. As Dominique Moisi has pointed out, last year's French presidential campaign saw "no reference . . . to the events of September 11 and their far-reaching consequences." No one asked, "What should be the role of France and Europe in the new configuration of forces created after September 11? How should France reappraise its military budget and doctrine to take account of the need to maintain some kind of parity between Europe and the United States, or at least between France and the UK?" The Middle East conflict became an issue in the campaign because of France's large Arab and Muslim population, as the high vote for Jean-Marie Le Pen demonstrated. But Le Pen is not a foreign policy hawk. And as Moisi noted, "For most French voters . . . security has little to do with abstract and distant geopolitics. Rather, it is a question of which politician can best protect them from the crime and violence plaguing the streets and suburbs of their cities."[52]

Can Europe change course and assume a larger role on the world stage? There has been no shortage of European leaders urging it to do so. Nor is the weakness of EU foreign policy today necessarily proof that it must be weak tomorrow, given the EU's record of overcoming weaknesses in other areas. And yet the political will to demand more power for Europe appears to be lacking, for the very good reason that Europe does not see a mission for itself that requires power. Its mission, if it has a mission beyond the confines of Europe, is to oppose power. It is revealing that the argument most often advanced by Europeans for augmenting their military strength is not that it will allow Europe to expand its strategic purview or even its global influence. It is merely to rein in and "multilateralize" the United States. "America," writes the pro-American British scholar Timothy Garton Ash, "has too much power for anyone's good, including its own."[53] Therefore Europe must amass power, but for no other reason than to save the world and the United States from the dangers inherent in the present lopsided situation.

Whether that particular mission is a worthy one or not, it seems unlikely to rouse European passions. Only France and Great Britain so far have responded even marginally to this challenge. But France's proposed defense budget increase will prove, like the *force de frappe*, more symbolic than real. Former French foreign minister Hubert

[52] Dominique Moisi, *Financial Times,* March 11, 2002.
[53] Timothy Garton Ash, *New York Times,* April 9, 2002.

Védrine, who once complained about American *hyper-puissance*, has stopped talking about counterbalancing the United States. Instead, he shrugs and declares there "is no reason for the Europeans to match a country that can fight four wars at once."[54] It was one thing for Europe in the 1990s to try to increase its annual collective expenditures on defense from $150 billion to $180 billion when the United States was spending $280 billion. But now that the United States is heading toward spending as much as $400 billion per year, or perhaps even more in coming years, Europe has not the slightest intention of keeping up. Thus France might increase its defense budget by 6 percent, prodded by the Gaullism of President Jacques Chirac. The United Kingdom might make an even greater commitment to strengthening and modernizing its military, guided by Tony Blair in an attempt to revive, if on a much smaller scale, an older British tradition of liberal imperialism. But what is "Europe" without Germany? And German defense budgets, today running at about the same percentage of gross domestic product as Luxembourg's, are destined to drop even further in coming years as the German economy struggles under the weight of a stifling labor and social welfare system. European analysts may lament the Continent's "strategic irrelevance." NATO Secretary General George Robertson may call Europe a "military pygmy" in a noble effort to shame Europeans into spending more, and more wisely than they do now. But who honestly believes Europeans will fundamentally change their way of doing business? They have many reasons not to.

[54] Quoted in David Ignatius, "France's Constructive Critic," *Washington Post*, February 22, 2002.

THE WORLD AMERICA MADE

If Americans are unhappy about this state of affairs, they should recall that today's Europe—both the integrated Europe and the weak Europe—is very much the product of American foreign policy stretching back over the better part of nine decades. The United States abandoned Europe after World War I, standing aside as the Continent slipped into a war even more horrible than the first. Even as World War II was ending, the initial American impulse was to walk away again. Franklin Delano Roosevelt's original wartime vision had been to make Europe strategically irrelevant.[55] In the late 1930s and even during the war, the common conviction of Americans was that "the European system was basically rotten, that war was endemic on that continent, and the Europeans had only themselves to blame for their plight."[56] Europe appeared to be nothing more than the overheated incubator of world wars that cost America dearly.

During World War II, Americans like Roosevelt, looking backward rather than forward, believed no greater service could be performed than to take Europe out of the global strategic picture once and for all. Roosevelt actually

[55] As the historian John Lamberton Harper has put it, FDR wanted "to bring about a radical reduction in the weight of Europe" and thereby make possible "the retirement of Europe from world politics." Harper, *American Visions of Europe: Franklin D. Roosevelt, George F. Kennan, and Dean G. Acheson* (Cambridge, UK, 1996), pp. 79, 3.

[56] William L. Langer and S. Everett Gleason, *The Challenge to Isolation, 1937–1940* (New York, 1952), p. 14.

preferred doing business with Stalin's Russia. "After Germany is disarmed," FDR pointedly asked, "what is the reason for France having a big military establishment?" Charles de Gaulle found such questions "disquieting for Europe and for France," as well he might have. Americans of Roosevelt's era held an old American view of Europe as corrupt and decadent, now mingled with a certain contempt for European weakness and dependence. If the European powers were being stripped of their global reach by military and economic weakness following the destruction of World War II, many Americans were only too happy to hurry the process along. As FDR had put it, "When we've won the war, I will work with all my might and main to see to it that the United States is not wheedled into the position of accepting any plan that will further France's imperialistic ambitions, or that will aid or abet the British Empire in its imperial ambitions."[57]

When the Cold War dawned, Americans such as Dean Acheson hoped to create in Europe a powerful partner against the Soviet Union, and most Americans who came of age during the Cold War have always thought of Europe almost exclusively in Achesonian terms—as the essential bulwark of freedom in the struggle against Soviet tyranny. But a suspicious hostility toward Europe always played around the edges of American foreign policy, even during the Cold War. When President Dwight Eisenhower undermined and humiliated Britain and France at Suez in 1956, it was only the most blatant of many American efforts to

---

[57] Quoted in Selig Adler, *The Isolationist Impulse: Its Twentieth-Century Reaction* (New York, 1957), p. 142; Kissinger, *Diplomacy*, p. 396.

cut Europe down to size and reduce its already weakened global influence.

Nevertheless, for the most part the emerging threat of the Soviet Union compelled Americans to recalculate their relationship with European security, and therefore with the Europeans. And ultimately the more important American contribution to Europe's current world-apart status stemmed not from anti-European but from essentially pro-European impulses. A commitment to Europe, not hostility to it, led the United States in the immediate postwar years to keep troops on the Continent and to create NATO. The presence of American forces as a security guarantee in Europe was, as it was intended to be, the critical ingredient for beginning the process of European integration so that a cohesive "West" would be strong enough materially and spiritually to withstand the daunting challenge of what promised to be a difficult Cold War confrontation with the Soviet Union.

Europe's evolution into its present state occurred under the mantle of the U.S. security guarantee and could not have occurred without it. Not only did the United States for almost half a century supply a shield against such external threats as the Soviet Union and internal threats posed by ethnic conflict in places like the Balkans. More important, the United States was the key to the solution of the "German problem" and perhaps still is. Germany's Fischer, in his Humboldt University speech, noted two "historic decisions" that made the new Europe possible: "the USA's decision to stay in Europe" and "France's and Germany's commitment to the principle of integration, beginning with economic links." But, of course, the latter could never have occurred without the former. France's willingness to risk the reintegration of Germany into Europe—and France was, to say the least, highly dubious—depended on the promise of continued American involvement in Europe as a guarantee against any resurgence of German militarism. Nor were postwar Germans unaware that their own future in Europe depended on the calming presence of the American military.

The current situation abounds in ironies. Europe's rejection of power politics and its devaluing of military force as a tool of international relations have depended on the presence of American military forces on European soil. Europe's new Kantian order could flourish only under the umbrella of American power exercised according to the rules of the old Hobbesian order. American power made it possible for Europeans to believe that power was no longer important. And now, in the final irony, the fact that U.S. military power has solved the European problem, especially the "German problem," allows Europeans today, and Germans in particular, to believe that American military power, and the "strategic culture" that has created and sustained it, is outmoded and dangerous.

Most Europeans do not see or do not wish to see the great paradox: that their passage into post-history has depended on the United States not making the same passage. Because Europe has neither the will nor the ability to guard its own paradise and keep it from being overrun, spiritually as well as physically, by a world that has yet to accept the rule of "moral consciousness," it has become dependent on America's willingness to use its military might to deter or defeat those around the world who still believe in power politics.

Some Europeans do understand the conundrum. Britons, not surprisingly, understand it best. Robert Cooper writes of the need to address the hard truth that although "within the postmodern world [i.e., the Europe of today], there are no security threats in the traditional sense," nevertheless, throughout the rest of the world—what Cooper calls the "modern and pre-modern zones"—threats abound. If the postmodern world does not protect itself, it can be destroyed. But how does Europe protect itself without discarding the very ideals and principles that undergird its pacific system?

"The challenge to the postmodern world," Cooper argues, "is to get used to the idea of double standards." Among themselves, Europeans may "operate on the basis of laws and open cooperative security." But when dealing with the world outside Europe, "we need to revert to the rougher methods of an earlier era—force, preemptive attack, deception, whatever is necessary." This is Cooper's principle for safeguarding society: "Among ourselves, we keep the law, but when we are operating in the jungle, we must also use the laws of the jungle." Cooper directs his argument at Europe, and he couples it with a call for Europeans to cease neglecting their defenses, "both physical and psychological."[58]

Cooper has also served as a close adviser to Tony Blair, and it is clear that Blair, perhaps a good deal more than

[58] Cooper, *The Observer,* April 7, 2002.

his Labour Party followers, has endorsed the idea of an international double standard for power. He has tried to lead Britain into the rule-based Kantian world of the European Union. But as his solidarity with President Bush on the question of Iraq has shown, Blair has also tried to lead Europe back out into the Hobbesian world, where military power remains a key feature of international relations.

But Blair's attempt to bring Europe along with him has been largely unsuccessful. Schroeder has taken his nation "the German way," and France, even under the more conservative Gaullism of Jacques Chirac, has been a most resistant partner of the United States, more intent on constraining American power than in supplementing it with French power.

One suspects that what Cooper has really described, therefore, is not Europe's future but America's present. For it is the United States that has had the difficult task of navigating between these two worlds, trying to abide by, defend, and further the laws of advanced civilized society while simultaneously employing military force against those who refuse to abide by such rules. The United States is already operating according to Cooper's double standard, for the very reasons he suggests. American leaders, too, believe that global security and a liberal order—as well as Europe's "postmodern" paradise—cannot long survive unless the United States does use its power in the dangerous Hobbesian world that still flourishes outside Europe.

What this means is that although the United States has played the critical role in bringing Europe into this Kantian paradise, and still plays a key role in making that paradise possible, it cannot enter the paradise itself. It mans the walls but cannot walk through the gate. The United States, with all its vast power, remains stuck in history, left to deal with the Saddams and the ayatollahs, the Kim Jong Ils and the Jiang Zemins, leaving most of the benefits to others.

IS IT STILL "THE WEST"?

If this evolving international arrangement continues to produce a greater American tendency toward unilateralism in international affairs, this should not surprise any objective observer. In return for manning the walls of Europe's postmodern order, the United States naturally seeks a certain freedom of action to deal with the strategic dangers that it alone has the means and sometimes the will to address. This is the great problem for relations between the United States and Europe, of course. For just at the moment when Europeans, freed of Cold War fears and constraints, have begun settling into their postmodern paradise and proselytizing for their doctrines of international law and international institutions, Americans have begun turning in the other direction, away from the common solidarity with Europe that had been the central theme of the Cold War and back toward a more traditional American policy of independence, toward that uniquely American form of universalistic nationalism.

The end of the Cold War had an even more profound effect on the transatlantic relationship than is commonly

understood, for the common Soviet enemy and the consequent need to act in concert for the common defense were
not all that disappeared after 1989. So, too, did a grand
strategy pursued on both sides of the Atlantic to preserve
and strengthen the cohesion and unity of what was called
"the West." It was not just that the United States and
Europe had had to work together to meet the Soviet challenge. More than that, the continued unity and success of
the liberal Western order was for many years the very definition of victory in the Cold War.

Partly for this reason, American strategy during the
Cold War often consisted of providing more to friends
and allies than was expected from them in return. To a
remarkable degree, American governments measured the
success of their foreign policy not by how well the United
States was doing by any narrow reckoning of the national
interest, but rather by how well America's allies were far-
ing against the many internal and external challenges they
faced. Thus it was American economic strategy to raise up
from the ruins of World War II powerful economic com-
petitors in Europe and Asia, even to the point where, by
the last decades of the Cold War, the United States seemed
to many to be in a state of relative decline compared to
its increasingly prosperous allies. It was American military strategy to risk nuclear attack upon its otherwise
unthreatened homeland in order to deter both nuclear
and conventional attacks on European and Asian allies.
When one considers the absence of similarly reliable guar-
antees among the various European powers in the past,
between, say, Great Britain and France in the 1920s and

1930s, the willingness of the United States, standing in relative safety behind two oceans, to link its very survival to that of other nations was rather extraordinary.

America's strategic and economic "generosity," if one can call it that, was, of course, closely related to American interests. As Acheson put it, "For the United States to take steps to strengthen countries threatened with Soviet aggression or Communist subversion . . . was to protect the security of the United States—it was to protect freedom itself."[59] But this identification of the interests of others with its own interests was a striking quality of American foreign and defense policy after World War II. After Munich, after Pearl Harbor, and after the onset of the Cold War, Americans increasingly embraced the conviction that their own well-being depended fundamentally on the well-being of others, that American prosperity could not occur in the absence of global prosperity, that American national security was impossible without a broad measure of international security. This was a doctrine of self-interest, but it was the most enlightened kind of self-interest—to the point where it was at times almost indistinguishable from idealism.

Almost, but never entirely. Idealism was never the sole source of American generosity or its propensity to seek to work in concert with its allies. American Cold War multilateralism was more instrumental than idealistic in its motives. After all, "going it alone" after 1945 meant going it alone against the Soviet Union. Going it alone meant shearing apart the West. Nor was it really conceivable,

[59] Quoted in Kissinger, *Diplomacy*, p. 452.

with Soviet troops massed in the heart of Europe, for any American foreign policy to succeed if it was not "multi-lateral" in its inclusion of Western European interests. On the other hand, genuine idealistic multilateralism had been interred for most Americans along with Wilson and the League of Nations Covenant. Dean Acheson, among the leading architects of the postwar international order, considered the UN Charter "impracticable" and the United Nations itself an example of a misguided Wilsonian "faith in the perfectibility of man and the advent of universal peace and law."[60] He and most others present at the creation of the postwar order were idealists, but they were practical idealists. They believed it was essential to present a common Western front to the Communist bloc, and if that meant swallowing what Acheson disparaged as the "holy writ" of the UN Charter, they were prepared to play along. For Acheson, support for the UN was nothing more than "an aid to diplomacy."[61] This is important, because many aspects of American behavior during the Cold War that both Europeans and many Americans in retrospect find so admirable, and whose passing they so lament, represented concessions made in the cause of Western unity.

That unity was not always easy to maintain. American hostility to de Gaulle's determined independence, American suspicion about British imperialism, arguments over Germany's *Ostpolitik,* strategic debates over arms agreements and arms buildups, especially during the Reagan years, all threatened to open cracks in the alliance. But

[60] Quoted in James Chace, *Acheson: The Secretary of State Who Created the American World* (New York, 1998), p. 107.

[61] Ibid., p. 108.

the cracks were always healed, because everyone agreed that while disagreements were inevitable, fissures were dangerous. If "the West" was divided, it would fall. The danger was not only strategic; it was ideological, even psychological. "The West" had to mean something, otherwise what were we defending? And, of course, during the Cold War, "the West" did mean something. It was the liberal, democratic choice of a large segment of humanity, standing in opposition to the alternative choice that existed on the other side of the Berlin Wall.

This powerful strategic, ideological, and psychological need to demonstrate that there was indeed a cohesive, unified West went down with the Berlin Wall and the statues of Lenin in Moscow. The loss was partly masked during the 1990s. Many saw the struggles in Bosnia and Kosovo as a new test of the West. The enlargement of NATO to include former Warsaw Pact nations was an ingathering of peoples who had been forcibly excluded from the West and wanted to be part of it again. They saw NATO as not only or even primarily a security organization but simply as the one and only institution that embodied the transatlantic West. Certainly, the United Nations was not "the West."

But the very success of the transatlantic project, the solution of the European security dilemma, the solution of the German problem, the completion of a Europe "whole and free," the settlement of the Balkan conflicts, the creation of a fairly stable zone of peace and democracy on the European continent—all these great and once unimaginable accomplishments had the inevitable effect of diminishing the significance of "the West." It was not that the West had ceased to exist. Nor was it that the West had ceased to face enemies, for surely militant Muslim fundamentalism is an implacable enemy of the West. But the central point of Francis Fukuyama's famous essay, "The End of History," was irrefutable: The centuries-long struggle among opposing conceptions of how mankind might govern itself had been definitively settled in favor of the Western liberal ideal. Muslim fundamentalism might have its following in the parts of the world where Muslims predominate. Nor can we doubt any longer its capacity to inflict horrific damage on the West. But as Fukuyama and others have pointed out, Muslim fundamentalism does not present a serious challenge to the universal principles of Western liberalism. The existence of Muslim fundamentalism may force Americans and Europeans to defend themselves against devastating attack, and even to cooperate in providing a common defense. But it does not force "the West" to prove itself unified and coherent, as Soviet communism once had.

With less need to preserve and demonstrate the existence of a cohesive "West," it was inevitable that the generosity that had characterized American foreign policy for fifty years would diminish after the Cold War ended. This may be something to lament, but it is not something to be surprised at. The existence of the Soviet Union and the international communist threat had disciplined Americans and made them see that their enlightened self-interest lay in a relatively generous foreign policy, especially toward Europe. After the end of the Cold War, that discipline was no longer present. The end of the Cold War subtly shifted the old equation between idealism and interest. Indeed, those who decry the decline of American generosity in the post–Cold War era must at least reckon with the logic of that decline. Since Americans objectively had less interest in a foreign policy characterized by generosity, for the United States to have maintained the same degree of generosity in its foreign policy as it had during the Cold War, the same commitment to international institutions, the same concern for and deference to allies, the American people would have had to become even more idealistic.

In fact, Americans are no more or less idealistic than they were fifty years ago. It is objective reality that has changed, not the American character. It was the changed international circumstances after the Cold War that opened the way to political forces in Congress, chiefly though not exclusively Republican, which aimed to rewrite old multilateral agreements and defeat new ones, to extricate the United States from treaty obligations now considered onerous or excessively intrusive into American sovereignty. What was new was not the existence of such forces and attitudes, for they had always been present in American politics. They had dominated American politics throughout the 1920s and 1930s, a period ushered in by a Republican president promising a "return to normalcy" after the ambitious idealism of the Wilson years. But during the Cold War, and especially during the years dominated by Republican presidents from Nixon to Reagan, the grand anti-communist strategy had overwhelmed such narrow nationalist sentiments and trumped concerns for sovereignty.

Nor was America's post–Cold War turn toward a more nationalist approach to foreign policy simply the product of a rising Republican Right. Realist international relations theorists and policymakers, the dominant intellectual force in the American foreign policy establishment, also pushed the United States back in the direction of a more narrow nationalism. They decried what Michael Mandelbaum famously called the "international social work" allegedly undertaken by the Clinton administration in Bosnia and Haiti. They insisted that the United States return to a more intent focus on the "national interest," now more narrowly defined than it had been during the Cold War. American realists from Brent Scowcroft to Colin Powell to James Baker to Lawrence Eagleburger did not believe the United States should take on the burden of solving the Balkan crisis or other "humanitarian" crises around the world. The Cold War was over, they argued, and it was therefore possible for American foreign policy to "return to normal."

Post–Cold War "normalcy," however, meant fewer concessions to international public opinion, less deference to allies, more freedom to act as the United States saw fit. These realists gave intellectual legitimacy to the forces in Congress who coupled talk of the "national interest" with calls for reductions in overseas involvements of all kind. If the "national interest" was to be narrowly conceived, many Republicans asked, why, exactly, was it still in the "national interest" for the United States to pay its comparatively exorbitant UN dues? A case that had been easier to make when the preservation of Western unity against communism was the goal of American foreign policy was now harder to make in the absence of such a far-reaching and enlightened definition of the American "national interest."

Even the Clinton administration, more idealistic and, perhaps ironically, more wedded to the Cold War foreign policy of generosity than the realists and Republicans, nevertheless could not escape the new post–Cold War reality. It was Clinton, after all, who ran for president in 1992 on a platform declaring that the American economy mattered and foreign policy did not. Clinton stepped in to try to repair "the West" only after trying desperately not to take on that responsibility. When the administration of George W. Bush came to office in January 2001, bringing with it the realist-nationalism of 1990s Republicanism, "the West" as a functioning concept in American foreign policy had become dormant. When the terrorists struck the United States eight months later, the Cold War equation was completely inverted. Now, with the threat brought directly to American soil, overleaping that of America's allies, the paramount issue was America's unique suffering and vulnerability, not "the West."

The declining significance of "the West" as an organizing principle of foreign policy was not just an American phenomenon, however. Post–Cold War Europe agreed that the issue was no longer "the West." For Europeans, the issue became "Europe." Proving that there was a united Europe took precedence over proving that there was a united West. A European "nationalism" mirrored the American nationalism, and although this was not Europe's intent, the present gap between the United States and Europe today may be traced in part to Europe's decision to establish itself as a single entity apart from the United States.

This effort impressed on American minds that the

transatlantic goal was no longer a unified West; the Europeans themselves no longer thought in such terms. Instead, Europeans spoke of "Europe" as another pole in a new multipolar world—a counterbalance to America. Europe would establish its own separate foreign policy and defense "identity" outside of NATO. The institutions Europeans revered were the European Union and the United Nations. But for Americans, as for Central and Eastern Europeans, the UN was not "the West," and the European Union was not "the West." Only NATO was "the West," and now Europeans were building an alternative to NATO. Everything the Europeans were doing made sense from a European perspective; and the project of European integration was objectively of benefit to the United States, at least insofar as it strengthened the peace. Nor was it the intention of most Europeans to raise a challenge to the United States, much less to the idea of "the West." But how surprising was it that Americans no longer placed as high a priority on the unity of the West and the cohesion of the alliance as they once had? Europeans had undertaken an all-consuming project in which the United States by definition could have no part. The United States, meanwhile, has projects of its own.

ADJUSTING TO HEGEMONY

America did not change on September 11. It only became more itself. Nor should there be any mystery about the course America is on, and has been on, not only over the past year or over the past decade, but for the better part of the past six decades, and, one might even say, for the better part of the past four centuries. It is an objective fact that Americans have been expanding their power and influence in ever-widening arcs since even before they founded their own independent nation. The hegemony that America established within the Western Hemisphere in the nineteenth century has been a permanent feature of international politics ever since. The expansion of America's strategic reach into Europe and East Asia that came with the Second World War has never been retracted. Indeed, it is somewhat remarkable to reflect that more than fifty years after the end of that war—a period that has seen Japanese and German enemies completely transformed into valued friends and allies—and more than a decade after the Cold War—which ended in another stunning transformation of a defeated foe—the United States nevertheless remains, and clearly intends to remain, the dominant strategic force in both East Asia and Europe. The end of the Cold War was taken by Americans as an opportunity not to retract but to expand their reach, to expand the alliance they lead eastward toward Russia, to strengthen their relations among the increasingly democratic powers of East Asia, to stake out interests in parts of the world, like Central Asia, that most Americans never knew existed before.

The myth of America's "isolationist" tradition is remarkably resilient. But it is a myth. Expansion of territory and influence has been the inescapable reality of American history, and it has not been an unconscious expansion. The ambition to play a grand role on the world stage is deeply rooted in the American character. Since independence and even before, Americans who disagreed on many things always shared a common belief in their nation's great destiny. Even as a weak collection of loosely united colonies stretched out across the Atlantic Coast, threatened on all sides by European empires and an untamed wilderness, the United States had appeared to its leaders a "Hercules in the cradle," "the embryo of a great empire." To the generation of the early republic, to Washington, Hamilton, Franklin, and Jefferson, nothing was more certain than that the North American continent would be subdued, American wealth and population would grow, and the young republic would someday come to dominate the Western Hemisphere and take its place among the world's great powers. Jefferson foresaw the establishment of a vast "empire of liberty." Hamilton believed America would, "erelong, assume an attitude correspondent with its great destinies—majestic, efficient, and operative of great things. A noble career lies before it."[62]

For those early generations of Americans, the promise of national greatness was not merely a comforting hope but an integral part of the national identity, inextricably entwined with the national ideology. The United States must become a great power, and perhaps the greatest power, they and many subsequent generations of Americans believed, because the principles and ideals upon which it was founded were unquestionably superior— superior not only to those of the corrupt monarchies of eighteenth- and nineteenth-century Europe, but to the ideas that had shaped nations and governments through-

[62] Quoted in Stourzh, *Alexander Hamilton*, p. 195.

out human history. The proof of the transcendent importance of the American experiment would be found not
only in the continual perfection of American institutions
at home but also in the spread of American influence in
the world. Americans have always been internationalists,
therefore, but their internationalism has always been a
by-product of their nationalism. When Americans sought
legitimacy for their actions abroad, they sought it not
from supranational institutions but from their own principles. That is why it was always so easy for so many Americans to believe, as so many still believe today, that by
advancing their own interests they advance the interests of
humanity. As Benjamin Franklin put it, America's "cause
is the cause of all mankind."[63]

This enduring American view of their nation's excep-
tional place in history, their conviction that their interests
and the world's interests are one, may be welcomed,
ridiculed, or lamented. But it should not be doubted. And
just as there is little reason to expect Europe to change its
fundamental course, there is little cause to believe the
United States will change its own course, or begin to conduct itself in the world in a fundamentally different manner. Absent some unforeseen catastrophe—not a setback
in Iraq or "another Vietnam," but a military or economic
calamity great enough to destroy the very sources of
American power—it is reasonable to assume that we have
only just entered a long era of American hegemony. Demo-
graphic trends show the American population growing

---

[63] Quoted in Edward Handler, *America and Europe in the Political
Thought of John Adams* (Cambridge, MA, 1964), p. 102.

faster and getting younger while the European population declines and steadily ages. According to *The Economist*, if present trends continue, the American economy, now roughly the same size as the European economy, could grow to be more than twice the size of Europe's by 2050. Today the median age of Americans is 35.5; in Europe it is 37.7. By 2050, the American median age will be 36.2. In Europe, if present trends persist, it will be 52.7. That means, among other things, that the financial burden of caring for elderly dependents will grow much higher in Europe than in the United States. And that means Europeans will have even less money to spend on defense in the coming years and decades than they do today. As *The Economist* observes, "The long-term logic of demography seems likely to entrench America's power and to widen existing transatlantic rifts," providing a stark "contrast between youthful, exuberant, multi-coloured America and ageing, decrepit, inward-looking Europe."[64]

If America's relative power will not diminish, neither are Americans likely to change their views of how that power is to be used. In fact, despite all the seismic geopolitical shifts that have occurred since 1941, Americans have been fairly consistent in their thinking about the nature of world affairs and about America's role in shaping the world to suit its interests and ideals. The founding document of the Cold War, Kennan's "Long Telegram," starkly set out the dominant perspective of America's postwar strategic culture: The Soviet Union was "impervious to the logic of reason," Kennan wrote, but would

[64] "Half a Billion Americans?," *The Economist*, August 22, 2002.

be "highly sensitive to the logic of force."[65] A good liberal Democrat like Clark Clifford agreed that the "language of military power" was the only language that the Soviets understood, and that the Soviet empire had to be considered a "distinct entity with which conflict is not predestined but with which we cannot pursue common goals."[66] Few Americans would put things that starkly today, but many Americans would agree with the sentiments. Last year large majorities of Democrats and Republicans in both houses of Congress agreed that the "language of military power" might be all that Saddam Hussein understood.

It is not that Americans never flirted with the kind of internationalist idealism that now permeates Europe. In the first half of the twentieth century, Americans fought Wilson's "war to end all wars," which was followed a decade later by an American secretary of state putting his signature to a treaty outlawing war. In the 1930s, Franklin Roosevelt put his faith in nonaggression pacts and asked merely that Hitler promise not to attack a list of countries Roosevelt presented to him. Even after the Yalta conference of 1945, a dying FDR could proclaim "the end of the system of unilateral action, the exclusive alliances, the spheres of influence, the balances of power," and to promise in their stead "a universal organization in which all peace-loving Nations will finally have a chance to join . . . a permanent structure of peace."[67] But Roosevelt no

[65] Quoted in Chace, *Acheson*, p. 150.
[66] Quoted in ibid., p. 157.
[67] Quoted in Kissinger, *Diplomacy*, p. 416.

longer had full confidence in such a possibility. After Munich and Pearl Harbor, and then, after a fleeting moment of renewed idealism, the plunge into the Cold War, Kennan's "logic of force" became the operating assumption of American strategy. Acheson spoke of building up "situations of strength" around the globe. The "lesson of Munich" came to dominate American strategic thought, and although it was supplanted for a brief time by the "lesson of Vietnam," today it remains the dominant paradigm. While a small segment of the American elite still yearns for "global governance" and eschews military force, Americans from Madeleine Albright to Donald Rumsfeld, from Brent Scowcroft to Anthony Lake, still remember Munich, figuratively if not literally. And for younger generations of Americans who do not remember Munich or Pearl Harbor, there is now September 11. One of the things that most clearly divides Europeans and Americans today is a philosophical, even metaphysical disagreement over where exactly mankind stands on the continuum between the laws of the jungle and the laws of reason. Americans do not believe we are as close to the realization of the Kantian dream as do Europeans.

So where do we go from here? Again, it is not hard to see where America is going. The September 11 attacks shifted and accelerated but did not fundamentally alter a course the United States was already on. They certainly did not alter but only reinforced American attitudes toward power. Recall that even before September 11, Acheson's successors were still, if somewhat distractedly, building "situations of strength" around the world. Before September 11, and indeed, even before the election of George

W. Bush, American strategic thinkers and Pentagon planners were looking ahead to the next strategic challenges that seemed likely to arise. One of those challenges was Iraq. During the Clinton years, Congress had passed by a nearly unanimous vote a bill authorizing military and financial support for Iraqi opposition forces, and the second Bush administration was considering plans to destabilize Iraq before the terrorists struck on September 11. The Clinton administration also laid the foundations for a new ballistic missile defense system to defend against rogue states such as Iraq, Iran, and North Korea. Had Al Gore been elected, and had there been no terrorist attacks on September 11, these programs—aimed squarely at Bush's "axis of evil"—would still be under way.

Americans before September 11 were augmenting, not diminishing, their military power. In the 2000 election campaign, Bush and Gore both promised to increase defense spending, responding not to any particular threat but only to the general perception that the American defense budget—then running at close to $300 billion per year—was inadequate to meet the nation's strategic requirements. American military and civilian leaders inside and outside the Pentagon were seized with the need to modernize American forces, to take advantage of what was and is regarded as a "revolution in military affairs" that could change the very nature of the way wars are fought. Behind this enthusiasm was a genuine concern that if the United States did not make the necessary investments in technological transformation, its forces, its security, and the world's security would be at risk in the future.

Before September 11, the American strategic community had begun to focus its attention on China. Few believed that a war with China was probable in the near future—unless as a result of some crisis over Taiwan— but many believed that some confrontation with China would become increasingly likely within the coming two decades, as China's military capacity and geopolitical ambitions grew. This concern about China was one of the driving forces behind the demand for technological modernization of the American military; it was, quietly, one of the motives behind the push for a new missile defense program; and in a broad sense it had already become an organizing principle of American strategic planning. The view of China as the next big strategic challenge took hold in the Clinton Pentagon, and was given official sanction by President Bush when he declared pointedly before and after his election that China was not a strategic partner but a strategic competitor of the United States.

When the Bush administration released its new National Security Strategy in September of last year, the ambitiousness of American strategy left many Europeans, and even some Americans, breathless. The new strategy was seen as a response to September 11, and perhaps in the minds of those who wrote it, it was. But the striking thing about that document is that aside from a few references to the idea of "pre-emption," which itself was hardly a novel concept, the Bush administration's "new" strategy was little more than a restatement of American policies, many going back a half century. The Bush strategy said nothing about the promotion of democracy abroad that had not been said with at least equal fervor by Harry Truman, John F. Kennedy, or Ronald Reagan. The declaration of

America's intent to remain the world's pre-eminent military power, and to remain strong enough to discourage any other power from challenging American pre-eminence, was merely the public expression of what had been an unspoken premise of American strategic planning—if not of actual defense spending and military capability—since the end of the Cold War.

The policies of the Clinton and Bush administrations, well or ill designed, nevertheless rested on a common and distinctly American assumption—that is, the United States as the "indispensable nation." Americans seek to defend and advance a liberal international order. But the only stable and successful international order Americans can imagine is one that has the United States at its center. Nor can Americans conceive of an international order that is not defended by power, and specifically by American power. If this is arrogance, at least it is not a new arrogance. Henry Kissinger once asked the aging Harry Truman what he wanted to be remembered for. Truman answered: "We completely defeated our enemies and made them surrender. And then we helped them to recover, to become democratic, and to rejoin the community of nations. Only America could have done that."[68] Even the most hardheaded American realists have grown sentimental contemplating what Reinhold Niebuhr once called America's "responsibility" for "solving . . . the world problem." George Kennan, setting forth his doctrine of containment—which he foresaw would be a terribly difficult strategy for a democracy to sustain—nevertheless saw

[68] Quoted in Kissinger, *Diplomacy*, p. 425.

the challenge as "a test of the overall worth of the United States as a nation among nations." He even suggested that Americans should express their "gratitude to a Providence which, by providing [them] with this implacable challenge, has made their entire security as a nation dependent on their pulling themselves together and accepting the responsibilities of moral and political leadership that history plainly intended them to bear."[69]

Americans are idealists. In some matters, they may be more idealistic than Europeans. But they have no experience of promoting ideals successfully without power. Certainly, they have no experience of successful supranational governance; little to make them place all their faith in international law and international institutions, much as they might wish to; and even less to let them travel, with the Europeans, beyond power. Americans, as good children of the Enlightenment, still believe in the perfectibility of man, and they retain hope for the perfectibility of the world. But they remain realists in the limited sense that they still believe in the necessity of power in a world that remains far from perfection. Such law as there may be to regulate international behavior, they believe, exists because a power like the United States defends it by force of arms. In other words, just as Europeans claim, Americans can still sometimes see themselves in heroic terms—as Gary Cooper at high noon. They will defend the townspeople, whether the townspeople want them to or not.

Today, as a result of the September 11 terrorist attacks,

[69] X [George F. Kennan], "The Sources of Soviet Conduct," p. 169.

the United States is embarked on yet another expansion of its strategic purview. Just as the Japanese attack on Pearl Harbor, which should not really have come as such a surprise, led to an enduring American role in East Asia and in Europe, so September 11, which future historians will no doubt depict as the inevitable consequence of American involvement in the Muslim world, will likely produce a lasting American military presence in the Persian Gulf and Central Asia, and perhaps a long-term occupation of one of the Arab world's largest countries. Americans may be surprised to find themselves in such a position, just as Americans of the 1930s would have been stunned to find themselves an occupying power in both Germany and Japan less than a decade later. But viewed from the perspective of the grand sweep of American history, a history marked by the nation's steady expansion and a seemingly ineluctable rise from perilous weakness to the present global hegemony, this latest expansion of America's strategic role may be less than shocking.

What does all this mean for the transatlantic relationship? Can Europe possibly follow where America leads? And if it cannot, does that matter?

One answer to these questions is that the crisis over Iraq has cast the transatlantic problem in the harshest possible light. When that crisis subsides, as in time it will, the questions of power that most divide Americans and Europeans may subside a bit as well; the common political culture and the economic ties that bind Americans and Europeans will then come to the fore—until the next international strategic crisis. But perhaps the next crisis will not bring out transatlantic disagreements as severely as the crisis over Iraq and the greater Middle East—a region where both American and European interests are great but where American and European differences have proved especially acute. The next international crisis could come in East Asia. Given its distance from Europe and the smaller European interest there, and the fact that Europeans could bring even less power to bear in East Asia than they can in the Middle East, thereby making them even less relevant to American strategic planning, it is possible that an Asian crisis would not lead to another transatlantic divide of the magnitude of that which we have been experiencing.

In short, although it is difficult to foresee a closing of the gap between American and European perceptions of the world, that gap may be more manageable than it currently appears. There need be no "clash of civilizations" within what used to be called "the West." The task, for both Europeans and Americans, is to readjust to the new reality of American hegemony. And perhaps, as the psychiatrists like to claim, the first step in managing this problem is to understand it and to acknowledge that it exists.

Certainly Americans, when they think about Europe, should not lose sight of the main point: The new Europe is indeed a blessed miracle and a reason for enormous celebration—on both sides of the Atlantic. For Europeans, it is the realization of a long and improbable dream: a continent free from nationalist strife and blood feuds, from military competition and arms races. War between the major European powers is almost unimaginable. After centuries of misery, not only for Europeans but also for those pulled into their conflicts—as Americans were twice in the past century—the new Europe really has emerged as a paradise. It is something to be cherished and guarded, not least by Americans, who have shed blood on Europe's soil and would shed more should the new Europe ever fail. This does not mean, however, that the United States can or should rely on Europe in the future as it has in the past. Americans should not let nostalgia for what may have been the unusual circumstances of the Cold War mislead them about the nature of their strategic relationship with the European powers in the post–Cold War era.

Can the United States prepare for and respond to the strategic challenges around the world without much help from Europe? The simple answer is that it already does. The United States has maintained strategic stability in Asia with no help from Europe. In the various crises in the Middle East and Persian Gulf over the past decade, including the present one, European help, even when enthusiastically offered, has been token. Whatever Europe can or cannot offer in terms of moral and political support, it has had little to offer the United States in strategic military terms since the end of the Cold War—except, of course, that most valuable of strategic assets, a Europe at peace.

Today the United States spends a little more than 3 percent of its GDP on defense. Were Americans to increase that to 4 percent—meaning a defense budget in excess of $500 billion per year—it would still represent a smaller percentage of national wealth than Americans spent on defense throughout most of the past half century. Even Paul Kennedy, who invented the term "imperial overstretch" in the late 1980s (when the United States was spending around 7 percent of its GDP on defense), believes the United States can sustain its current military spending levels and its current global dominance far into the future. The United States can manage, therefore, at least in material terms. Nor can one argue that the American people are unwilling to shoulder this global burden, since they have done so for a decade already, and after September 11 they seem willing to continue doing so for a long time to come. Americans apparently feel no resentment at not being able to enter Europe's "postmodern" world. There is no evidence that most Americans desire to. Partly because they are so powerful, they take pride in their nation's military power and their nation's special role in the world.

The dangers of the present transatlantic predicament, then, lie neither in American will nor capability, but in the inherent moral tension of the current international situation. As is so often the case in human affairs, the real question is one of intangibles—of fears, passions, and beliefs. The problem is that the United States must sometimes play by the rules of a Hobbesian world, even though in doing so it violates Europe's postmodern norms. It must refuse to abide by certain international conventions that may constrain its ability to fight effectively in Robert Cooper's jungle. It must support arms control, but not always for itself. It must live by a double standard. And it must sometimes act unilaterally, not out of a passion for unilateralism but only because, given a weak Europe that has moved beyond power, the United States has no choice *but* to act unilaterally.

Few Europeans admit, as Cooper does implicitly, that such American behavior may redound to the greater benefit of the civilized world, that American power, even employed under a double standard, may be the best means of advancing human progress—and perhaps the only means. As Niebuhr wrote a half century ago, America's "inordinate power," for all its "perils," provides "some real advantages for the world community."[70] Instead, many Europeans today have come to consider the United States itself to be the outlaw, a rogue colossus. The danger—if it is a danger—is that the United States and Europe could become positively estranged. Europeans could become more and more shrill in their attacks on the United States. The United States could become less inclined to listen, or perhaps even to care. The day could come, if it has not already, when Americans might no more heed the pronouncements of the EU than they do the pronouncements of ASEAN or the Andean Pact.

To those of us who came of age in the Cold War, the strategic decoupling of Europe and the United States seems frightening. De Gaulle, when confronted by FDR's vision of a world where Europe was irrelevant, recoiled and suggested that this vision "risked endangering the Western world." If Western Europe was to be considered a "secondary matter" by the United States, would not FDR only "weaken the very cause he meant to serve—that of civilization?" Western Europe, de Gaulle maintained, was "essential to the West. Nothing can replace the value, the power, the shining example of the ancient peoples." Typically, he insisted this was "true of France above all."[71]

[70] Reinhold Niebuhr, *The Irony of American History* (New York, 1962), p. 134

[71] Quoted in Harper, *American Visions of Europe*, pp. 114–15.

But leaving aside French *amour propre*, did not de Gaulle have a point? If Americans were to decide that Europe was no more than an irritating irrelevancy, would American society gradually become unmoored from what we now call "the West"? It is not a risk to be taken lightly, on either side of the Atlantic.

So what is to be done? The obvious answer is that Europe should follow the course that Cooper, Ash, Robertson, and others recommend and build up its military capabilities, even if only marginally. There is not much ground for hope that this will happen. But, then, who knows? Maybe concern about America's overweening power really will create some energy in Europe. Perhaps the atavistic impulses that still swirl in the hearts of Germans, Britons, and Frenchmen—the memory of power, international influence, and national ambition—can still be played upon. Some Britons still remember empire; some Frenchmen still yearn for *la gloire;* some Germans still want their place in the sun. These urges are now mostly channeled into the grand European project, but they could find more traditional expression. Whether this is to be hoped for or feared is another question. It would be better still if Europeans could move beyond fear and anger at the rogue colossus and remember, again, the vital necessity of having a strong, even predominant America— for the world and especially for Europe. It would seem to be an acceptable price to pay for paradise.

Americans can help. It is true that the Bush administration came into office with something of a chip on its shoulder. The realist-nationalist impulses it inherited from the Republican Congress of the 1990s made it appear almost eager to scorn the opinions of much of the rest of the world. The picture it painted in its early months was of a behemoth thrashing about against constraints that only it could see. It was hostile to the new Europe—as to a lesser extent was the Clinton administration—seeing it not so much as an ally but as an albatross. Even after September 11, when the Europeans offered their very limited military capabilities in the fight in Afghanistan, the United States resisted, fearing that European cooperation was a ruse to tie America down. The Bush administration viewed NATO's historic decision to aid the United States under Article 5 less as a boon than as a booby trap. An opportunity to draw Europe into common battle out in the Hobbesian world, even in a minor role, was thereby unnecessarily squandered.

But Americans are powerful enough that they need not fear Europeans, even when bearing gifts. Rather than viewing the United States as a Gulliver tied down by Lilliputian threads, American leaders should realize that they are hardly constrained at all, that Europe is not really capable of constraining the United States. If the United States could move past the anxiety engendered by this inaccurate sense of constraint, it could begin to show more understanding for the sensibilities of others, a little more of the generosity of spirit that characterized American foreign policy during the Cold War. It could pay its respects to multilateralism and the rule of law, and try to build some international political capital for those moments when multilateralism is impossible and unilateral action unavoidable. It could, in short, take more care to show what the founders called a "decent respect for the opinion of mankind." This was always the wisest policy. And there is certainly benefit in it for the United States: Winning the material and moral support of friends and allies, especially in Europe, is unquestionably preferable to acting alone in the face of European anxiety and hostility.

These are small steps, and they will not address the deep problems that beset the transatlantic relationship today. But, after all, it is more than a cliché that the United States and Europe share a set of common Western beliefs. Their aspirations for humanity are much the same, even if their vast disparity of power has now put them in very different places. Perhaps it is not too naïvely optimistic to believe that a little common understanding could still go a long way.

American Power and the Crisis of Legitimacy

"WHAT KIND OF WORLD order do we want?" That question, posed by Germany's foreign minister, Joschka Fischer, on the eve of the American invasion of Iraq in March 2003, has been on the minds of many Europeans these days.[1] That by itself shows the differences that separate Europeans and Americans today, for it is safe to say the great majority of Americans have not pondered the question of "world order" since the war.

They will have to. The great transatlantic debate over the Iraq war was rooted in profound disagreement over "world order." Yes, Americans and Europeans differed on the specific question of what to do about Iraq. They debated whether Saddam Hussein posed a serious threat and whether war was the right answer. A solid majority of Americans answered yes to both questions; even larger majorities of Europeans answered no. But these disagreements reflected more than simple tactical and analytical assessments of the situation in Iraq. As France's foreign minister, Dominique de Villepin, put it, the struggle was

---

[1] Joschka Fischer interview in *Der Spiegel*, March 24, 2003.

not so much about Iraq as it was a conflict between "two visions of the world."[2] The differences in Iraq were not only about policy. They were also about first principles. Opinion polls taken before, during, and after the war have shown two peoples living on separate strategic and ideological planets. More than 80 percent of Americans believe war may achieve justice; less than half of Europeans believe that a war—any war—can ever be just.[3] Americans and Europeans disagree about the role of international law and international institutions, and about the nebulous and abstract yet powerful question of international legitimacy. These different worldviews predate the Iraq war and the presidency of George W. Bush, although both the war and the Bush administration's conduct of international affairs have deepened and perhaps hardened this transatlantic rift into an enduring feature of the international landscape. "America is different from Europe," Gerhard Schroeder declared matter-of-factly months before the war.[4] Who any longer can deny it?[5]

[2] Dominique de Villepin, address to the UN Security Council, March 19, 2003.

[3] See *Transatlantic Trends 2003*, a survey commissioned by the German Marshall Fund of the United States and the Compagnia di San Paolo. Polling was conducted June 10–25, 2003, in eight countries: the United States, France, Germany, Great Britain, Italy, the Netherlands, Poland, and Portugal. (Results can be viewed at www.transatlantictrends. org.)

[4] Gerhard Schroeder interview in *The New York Times*, September 4, 2002.

[5] As the British political scientist Christopher Croker has observed, "Nothing is more naïve than the claim that the rifts are likely to end if Bush fails to be reelected in 2004 or if the Schroeder government loses power." Christopher Croker, *Empires in Conflict: The Growing Rift*

When this book was first published at the beginning of 2003, before the Iraq war, the transatlantic gulf was plainly visible. Less clear then, however, was how significant it would turn out to be for the world. One could imagine a transatlantic parting of the ways on global strategic matters that was, if not quite amicable, at least manageable, a strategic division of labor in which Europe concentrated on Europe and the United States on everything else. Cold War strategic partnership might be replaced by a certain mutual indifference, but that need not augur an ongoing crisis within the West. Could not Americans and Europeans simply say to one another, in the words of Bob Dylan, "You go your way, and I'll go mine"?

Today a darker possibility looms. A great philosophical schism has opened within the West, and instead of mutual indifference, mutual antagonism threatens to debilitate both sides of the transatlantic community. Coming at a time in history when new dangers and crises are proliferating rapidly, this schism could have serious consequences. For Europe and the United States to decouple strategically has been bad enough. But what if the schism over "world order" infects the rest of what we have known as the liberal West? Will the West still be the West?

A few years ago such questions were unthinkable. After the Cold War, Francis Fukuyama assumed, along with the rest of us, that at the end of history the world's liberal democracies would live in relative harmony. Conflicts would be between the West and "the rest," not within the

---

Between Europe and the United States, Whitehall Paper 58 (London, 2003): 3.

West itself. The world's democracies, sharing common liberal, democratic principles, would "have no grounds on which to contest each other's legitimacy."[6] That reasonable assumption has been thrown into doubt. For it is precisely the question of legitimacy that is at issue today between Americans and Europeans—not the legitimacy of each other's political institutions, perhaps, but of their differing visions of "world order."[7] More to the point, it is the legitimacy of American power and American global leadership that has come to be doubted by a majority of Europeans. America, for the first time since World War II, is suffering a crisis of international legitimacy.

Americans will find that they cannot ignore this problem. The struggle to define and obtain international legitimacy in this new era may prove to be among the critical contests of our time, in some ways as significant in determining the future of the international system and America's place in it as any purely material measure of power and influence.

THE THREE PILLARS OF COLD WAR LEGITIMACY

Where exactly has this struggle over legitimacy come from? Throughout the Cold War the legitimacy of Ameri-

[6] Francis Fukuyama, *The End of History and the Last Man* (New York, 1992), p. 263.

[7] Actually, Europeans and Americans do at times question each other's political and economic institutions.

can power and global leadership was largely taken for granted, and not just by Americans. The vast majority of Europeans, though they sometimes chafed under American dominance and often questioned American actions in Vietnam, Latin America, and elsewhere, nevertheless accepted American leadership as both necessary and desirable.

Contrary to much mythologizing on both sides of the Atlantic these days, the foundations of America's Cold War legitimacy had little if anything to do with the fact that the United States created the United Nations or faithfully abided by the precepts of international law as laid out in the UN Charter. The UN Security Council was paralyzed for the first four decades of its existence by the Cold War confrontation. The United States did not consider itself bound to seek the approval of the Security Council before making or threatening war, and Europeans neither expected nor demanded that it should. Nor did European nations themselves seek such authorization when they went to war in the Middle East or in Southeast Asia or in the South Atlantic. When the United States did cite international law to justify its Cold War policies, it appealed to the catch-all principle of collective self-defense—based on the sometimes dubious proposition that any action taken by the United States, from military interventions to clandestine overthrows of regimes throughout the third world, was by definition an act of collective defense of the "free world" against an inherently aggressive international communism.

It was not a structure of rules, laws, and institutions but the circumstances of the Cold War and America's special role in that conflict that provided the United States with legitimacy, at least within the West.[8] In Europe, American legitimacy rested on three pillars, all based on the existence of a Soviet communist empire.

The sturdiest pillar was the common strategic threat of the Soviet Union—the reality made vivid daily by hundreds of thousands of Soviet troops parked in the center of Europe. Coupled with this common threat was the common understanding that only the United States possessed the power to deter it. For most Europeans, and for most of America's Asian allies, too, America's widely agreed-upon role as principal defender against the Soviet threat gave it a very broad mantle of legitimacy. Even when Europeans believed the United States was acting foolishly or immorally, as in Vietnam, most nevertheless continued to accept American power and global leadership—partly because they had to. Much of the legitimacy the United States enjoyed within the West during the Cold War derived from the self-interest of its allies.

Complementing the common strategic threat was a common ideological threat. During the Cold War the United States prided itself on being the "leader of the free world" against the totalitarian world, and most Europeans agreed. The Cold War's Manichean struggle provided the world's most powerful democracy substantial authority in the democratic camp. In retrospect it is clear that commonly shared liberal democratic principles meant a good

[8] Outside of Europe and Japan, in places such as Latin America, the Middle East, and Africa, and of course Russia and China, America was generally accorded less legitimacy.

deal more in a world threatened by totalitarianism than they would in a world made safer for democracy.

Finally, the Cold War's "bipolar" international system provided what might be called a structural legitimacy. The roughly equal balance between the two superpowers meant that America's power, though vast, was nevertheless checked. It was not that Europeans welcomed Soviet military power on the continent. But many implicitly understood that the existence of Soviet conventional and nuclear power acted as a restraint on the Americans. De Gaulle's France, Willy Brandt's Germany, and others relished the small measure of independence from American dominance that the superpower balance gave them.

At the end of the Cold War these pillars of American legitimacy fell to the ground along with the Berlin Wall and the statues of Lenin. There has been little in the post–Cold War era to replace them. Radical, militant Islam, whatever dangers it may represent when manifested as terrorism, has not and cannot replace communism as an *ideological* threat to Western liberal democracy. Today, the phrase "leader of the free world" sounds vaguely absurd even to American ears.

Nor has the massive threat of the Soviet Union been replaced as a source of American legitimacy by the more diffuse and opaque threats of the post–Cold War era. Ethnic conflict in the Balkans in the 1990s compelled Europeans to give their blessing to American military intervention, and making Europe "whole and free" was a transatlantic project in which America was still accorded a leadership role, especially by the nations of Central and Eastern Europe. But the completion of that project put an end to European strategic dependence on the United States, at least in the view of many Western Europeans. The peoples of Europe never fully shared American concerns about weapons of mass destruction in Iraq, Iran, and North Korea, not during the Clinton administration nor afterward. Nor do most Europeans today share Americans' post–September 11 alarm over the possible nexus between such weapons and international terrorism. Rightly or wrongly, in their hearts, Europeans do not believe those weapons will be aimed at them. And to the extent that Europeans do worry, most no longer look to the United States to protect them. Europeans living in their geopolitical paradise do not fear the jungles beyond; therefore they no longer welcome those who guard the gates. Instead, they ask: Who will guard the guards?

America's legitimacy during the Cold War rested heavily on European self-interest. Today Europeans' relative strategic independence has caused many to take back the blanket legitimacy they once accorded America.[9] Indeed, the disappearance of the Soviet threat, the inauguration of the present "unipolar" international system, and the consequent loss of structural legitimacy have turned many Europeans' fears and suspicions westward across the Atlantic. Far from viewing the United States as a protector and therefore a legitimate "leader," many Euro-

[9] The exception, of course, is in Eastern and Central Europe, where most nations still feel strategically dependent on the United States. But if and as these powers feel less threatened over the coming years, and as they become more entangled in the European Union's web of economic and political relationships, they may follow the path of the Western European peoples.

peans today worry about an unconstrained America that has grown beyond their control.

THE UNIPOLAR PREDICAMENT

What might be called the "unipolar predicament," therefore, is not the product of any specific American policy or of a particular American administration. With the end of the Cold War, America's unprecedented global power itself has unavoidably become the new issue, one with which Europeans and Americans have only in begun to grapple.

"What do we do," Joschka Fischer asked after the Iraq war began, "when . . . our most important partner is making decisions that we consider extremely dangerous?"[10] What indeed? The question is a relatively new one, because the loss of European control over American actions is a relatively new phenomenon. During the Cold War, even a dominant United States was compelled to listen to the Europeans, if only because American Cold War policy aimed above all else at protecting and strengthening Europe. Today, Europe has lost much of the influence it once enjoyed. It is too weak to be an essential ally, and it is too secure to be a potential victim. Whereas during the Cold War the United States used to calculate how its actions would affect Europe's security, today it does not have to worry nearly as much.

That's why Europeans are worried—about unconstrained American power and about how they can regain

[10] Fischer interview in *Der Spiegel*, March 24, 2003.

113

some control over how the United States exercises that power. For one thing, Europeans too long have been accustomed to shaping the world, either through their own power or through their influence over the Americans, to sit back happily now and let America do the driving alone. And what are Europeans to do if they believe the United States is driving dangerously? Europeans felt this loss of control acutely during the Balkan conflicts of the 1990s, when in the early part of the decade they waited helplessly for a hesitant Clinton administration to act. Then, when the United States did act, in the 1999 Kosovo war, they had to watch as that difficult conflict in their own backyard was directed almost entirely by an American general. Whether the American president was George Bush, Bill Clinton, or George W. Bush, the new international structure has put Europeans in the unenviable position of having to trust the sole superpower to judge and act wisely. That isn't an easy thing to do, for as Europeans well know, all nations make bad judgments sometimes.

The unipolar predicament raises even more fundamental issues, however. Above all, it raises the issue of political and moral legitimacy. To the modern liberal mind, there is something inherently illegitimate about the idea of a single, dominant world power unconstrained except by its own sense of restraint. No matter how diplomatically adept an American president might be, the spirit of liberal democracy recoils from the idea of hegemonic dominance, domestic as well as international, no matter how benignly it may be exercised. As Kenneth N. Waltz put it in a 1997 essay, "Unbalanced power, whoever wields it, is a potential danger to others."[11] Nature, most assume, abhors a monopoly of power as much as it does a vacuum of power.[12] And is it not true, as Lord Acton wrote, that absolute power corrupts absolutely?

To the Western liberal mind, checks and balances are prerequisites for justice and freedom in domestic life. As the British scholar-statesman Robert Cooper argues, "Our domestic systems are designed to place restraint on power. . . . We value pluralism and the rule of law domestically and it is difficult for democratic societies—including the USA—to escape from the idea that they are desirable internationally as well."[13] Would the United States use its power to serve its own narrow interests, at the expense of others? That is what worries even friends and admirers of the United States these days. "The difficulty with the American monopoly of force in the world community," Cooper argues, "is that it is American and will be exercised, necessarily, in the interests of the United States. This will not be seen as legitimate."[14]

---

[11] Kenneth N. Waltz, "Evaluating Theories," *American Political Science Review* 91 (December 1997): 915.

[12] In fact, according to realist and neo-realist theory, a unipolar world of the kind we now live in is impossible, or at least is inherently unstable and short-lived, because the emergence of a sole superpower must quickly lead the world's other powers to band together in opposition and restore international balance. For a summary and refutation of this theory, see William C. Wohlforth, "The Stability of a Unipolar World," *International Security* 24 (Summer 1999): 5–41.

[13] Robert Cooper, *The Breaking of Nations*, (London, 2003), pp. 163–64.

[14] Cooper, *The Breaking of Nations*, p. 167.

Well before the Bush administration proved so maladroit at reassuring even America's closest allies, other post–Cold War administrations had faced mounting anxiety about America's growing dominance. In the 1990s, while Bill Clinton and Madeleine Albright were proudly dubbing the United States the "indispensable nation," French foreign ministers, along with their Russian and Chinese counterparts, were declaring the American-led unipolar world to be unjust and dangerous. In the Clinton years, Samuel P. Huntington was warning about the "arrogance" and "unilateralism" of American policies, and European complaints about the "arrogance" and "bullying" of the Clinton administration before, during, and after the Kosovo war in 1999 evinced a growing concern about the inherent problems of the new structure, and especially the accelerating loss of European control.[15]

For many Europeans the nightmare became real after September 11, 2001. For after the attack on the United States, the Bush administration and Americans generally became quite frank about wielding American power primarily if not exclusively in defense of their own newly endangered vital interests. The initial European support for the American invasion in Afghanistan, and the historic invocation of Article V by the NATO allies, providing for a collective defense of the United States, were aimed in part at ensuring the United States did not go off on its own and at giving Europe some control over the American

[15] As Huntington noted, "political and intellectual leaders in most countries strongly resist the prospect of a unipolar world and favor the emergence of true multipolarity." See Samuel P. Huntington, "The Lonely Superpower," *Foreign Affairs* 78 (March/April 1999): 34.

response to the terrorist attacks. That was one reason why America's apparent indifference to these offers of assistance was so troubling to Europeans. Then when the United States began looking beyond Afghanistan, toward Iraq and an "axis of evil," Europeans realized they had lost control. The Cold War bargain underlying transatlantic cooperation had become inverted. Whereas once the United States risked its own safety in defense of a threatened Europe's vital interests, today a threatened America looks out for itself in apparent and sometimes genuine disregard for what many Europeans perceive to be *their* moral, political, and security interests.

For Europeans the problem of American hegemony has been especially vexing because there is so little they can do about it. Since the 1990s hopes for an emerging multipolar world have faded. Today almost everyone concedes the near impossibility of matching American power for decades to come, and even then the most likely candidates to compete with American power, China and Russia, do not offer an attractive prospect for most Europeans. Europe's own military capabilities continue to decline relative to the United States, and French ambitions to create a European counterweight to the United States are constantly overwhelmed by the more powerful, postmodern European aversion to military power, to power politics, and to the very idea of the balance of power.[16] They

[16] Indeed, there is something contradictory in Europeans seeking a return to a global balance of power, in order to restore peace and justice to the international system, when they have rejected the balance of power as the greatest threat to peace and justice on the continent of Europe.

have been checked, too, by fears of alienating the powerful United States, mingled with widespread European suspicions of France's "soft" hegemonism and lingering fears of renewed German power.

In the end, however, Europeans have not sought to counter American hegemony in the usual, power-oriented fashion because they do not find American hegemony threatening in the traditional power-oriented way. Kenneth N. Waltz was wrong in this respect: Not all global hegemons are equally frightening. The danger posed by the United States, as Europeans well know, is not to European security or even to European independence and autonomy.[17] The American "threat" is of an entirely different nature. What Europeans fear is not that the United States wants to control them but that they have lost control of the United States and, therefore, by extension, of the direction of world affairs.

If the United States is suffering a crisis of legitimacy today, the European desire to regain some measure of control over American behavior is a large part of the reason.[18] The vast majority of Europeans objected to the American invasion of Iraq not only because they opposed the war. It was America's willingness and ability to go to

[17] For all the talk about American "empire," Europeans know that the United States does not have imperial ambitions to control the continent of Europe as would-be hegemons have tried in the past, from Louis XIV to Napoleon to Hitler.

[18] Again, the fact that Russia, China, and many nations of Latin America, Africa, and the Middle East opposed the use of American power as illegitimate is not a new phenomenon. What is new and dramatic is the defection of America's European allies to that camp.

war without the approval of the Security Council, which is also to say, without the approval of all Europe, that posed the greater challenge both to the European view of world order and to Europe's ability to exercise even a modicum of influence in the new unipolar system. "A world order cannot function when the national interest of the strongest power is the definitive criterion for the use of that country's power," Joschka Fischer complained. There must be rules to govern the behavior of all nations, he insisted, and these rules "must apply to the big, the medium-sized, and the small nations."[19] As President Jacques Chirac put it, world crises cannot be addressed "by one nation acting alone on the basis of its own interests and judgments. . . . Any crisis situation, regardless of its nature, in any part of the world, is of concern to the whole international community."[20] In these calls for the involvement of the "international community" there is an unmistakable insistence that Europe, in particular, be given a hand on the tiller.

This is not to argue that the European demand that the United States seek international legitimization for its actions is cynical. Because of their own history, and because Europeans now operate within an international organization, the European Union, that requires multilateral agreement on all matters, the European commitment to a legitimacy derived from multilateral negotiation and international legal institutions is sincere, even zealous. But ideals and self-interest frequently coincide, and European

---

[19] Fischer interview in *Der Spiegel*, March 24, 2003.
[20] Jacques Chirac, televised interview, July 14, 2003.

assaults on the legitimacy of American actions and American power may be an effective if unconventional way of constraining and controlling the American superpower. Legitimacy, writes Cooper, "is as much a source of power as force," and many Europeans undoubtedly hope that this is true.

Certainly "legitimacy" is an asset Europeans believe they have in abundance. It is their comparative advantage in the new geopolitical jostling with the United States, the great equalizer in an otherwise lopsided relationship. The European Union, most of its members believe, enjoys a natural legitimacy, simply by virtue of the fact that it is a collective body. There is both strength and legitimacy in numbers, and in a modern liberal world this legitimacy is something that can be wielded as a substitute for other types of power. It can also be bartered for influence. The United States needs Europe, argues Javier Solana, because Europe is "a partner with the legitimacy that comes through the collective action of a union of twenty-five sovereign states."[21] In return for a greater say in world affairs and greater control of America's exercise of power, Europe can give the United States the legitimacy it now lacks. For many Europeans, in fact, this is the new grand bargain for the unipolar era. Joschka Fischer predicts that Americans will discover in Iraq that "the question of legitimization goes beyond the capabilities of the U.S."[22] But this is more than a prediction. It is also a European bid for influence.

That does not mean that Fischer is wrong, however. He

[21] Javier Solana, "The Future of Transatlantic Relations: Reinvention or Reform?" *Progressive Governance*, July 10, 2003.

[22] Fischer interview, *Die Zeit*, May 8, 2003.

is probably right. The experiment of attempting to invade and then reconstruct Iraq without the broad benediction of Europe has not been a particularly happy one, even if the United States eventually succeeds in Iraq. The United States cannot ignore the question of legitimacy, nor is international legitimacy something the United States can provide itself. So if the United States needs legitimacy, where should it look to find it?

THE MYTH OF "INTERNATIONAL ORDER"

Since the United States first began openly contemplating the invasion of Iraq, the European answer has been the UN Security Council. "It is from the United Nations alone that the legal and moral authority can come," Dominique de Villepin insisted before, during, and after the war.[23] And there is no doubt that the French foreign minister speaks for the vast majority of Europeans, including Britons, Spaniards, Poles, and Italians and many others in the mis-named "new Europe." Indeed, so powerful is this conviction throughout all of Europe that even America's staunchest ally, Tony Blair, the leader of America's least "European" transatlantic partner, Great Britain, nevertheless considered UN authorization for the invasion of Iraq absolutely essential to satisfy his own public.[24] Presi-

[23] De Villepin address to the UN Security Council, March 19, 2003.
[24] So much so that he sacrificed a great deal of his personal and international political capital in the futile attempt to gain a second resolution explicitly authorizing war.

dent Bush's decision to turn to the United Nations was very much driven by Blair's political needs in the United Kingdom and also by Blair's need for influence on the European continent. "The United Nations is the place where international rules and legitimacy are founded," de Villepin declared at the Security Council in March, "because it speaks in the name of peoples."[25]

Nor is this conviction to be found only in Europe. Americans have a certain reverence for the UN Security Council, too, as polls consistently show. American support is significantly more measured and a good deal more conditional than that of the Europeans, of course: A solid majority of Americans favored bypassing the UN Security Council to invade Iraq.[26] But there is enough support for the United Nations that George W. Bush decided it was wise, at least for the sake of appearances, to seek the Security Council's approval for the Iraq war, and then to return to the Security Council again and again since the war in pursuit of international support—and international legitimacy.

But are the UN Security Council, and the structure of international law it sits atop, really the holy grail of international legitimacy, as Europeans are today insisting? International life would be simpler if they were. But they are not. Ever since the UN was founded almost six decades ago, the Security Council has never functioned as its more idealistic authors intended. Nor in all that time has it been recognized and accepted as the sole source of interna-

---

[25] De Villepin address to the UN Security Council, March 19, 2003.
[26] See *Transatlantic Trends 2003*.

tional legitimacy—not even by Europeans. Indeed, the European demand that the United States seek UN authorization of the Iraq war, and presumably for all future wars, has been a novel, even revolutionary, proposal.

For most of the UN's existence, during the four decades of the Cold War, the Security Council was paralyzed by the implacable hostility between its two strongest, veto-wielding members. Only after the fall of the Soviet Union and the end of the Cold War was it even possible to imagine the Security Council functioning as the sole locus for international authority and legitimacy. Many then hoped that the UN, which was essentially "a pre–Cold War institution," might therefore "become a workable post–Cold War institution."[27]

But the record of the post–Cold War years has been spotty. The first President Bush sought and gained the Security Council's approval in the first Persian Gulf war in 1991, but only after deploying 500,000 troops and making clear that the United States would act without authorization if it had to.[28] The Clinton administration sent troops to Haiti in 1994 without the Security Council's authorization, which came after the fact. In 1998 the Clinton administration bombed Iraq in Operation Desert Fox without a resolution and, indeed, over strong objections registered in the Security Council by France and Russia. There were occasions when the Security Council functioned, but most observers agree that its authority weakened rather

[27] Cooper, *The Breaking of Nations,* p. 57.
[28] Had the Soviet Union blocked a resolution authorizing the first Gulf war, no one, including the Soviets, believed Bush would have brought his half million troops back home.

than strengthened over the course of the first decade after
the Cold War.

The most interesting case was Kosovo. For in Kosovo it
was the Europeans who, along with the United States,
went to war without obtaining the legitimizing sanction
of the UN Security Council.[29] Nevertheless, most Europeans at the time and ever since have insisted that the
Kosovo war was legitimate. They believed Europe in particular had a moral responsibility to prevent another
genocide on the European continent. Nor was it an acci-
dent that among the strongest proponents of war in 1999
was a German, Joschka Fisher, the head of the intensely
moralistic Green Party. For Fischer, as for Gerhard
Schroeder and Tony Blair, the dire humanitarian emergency and the brutal behavior of the Serbs overrode the
legal requirement for UN authorization. The European
response to Kosovo, Robert Cooper writes, was driven by
"the collective memory of the holocaust and the streams
of displaced people created by extreme nationalism in the
Second World War," and this "common historical experience" provided "justification for armed intervention." The
fact that this potential genocide was occurring in Europe
gave Europeans not only special responsibility, but also
special license to go to war to stop it. History and morality
trumped traditional principles of international law. "It
would be a very different thing," Cooper noted, in a book
written after the Iraq war, for Europe "to intervene in
another continent with another history." The "European

[29] When NATO went to war against Serbia in 1999, the allies tried
but failed to obtain authorization because Russia, Serbia's historic protector, opposed the war.

order is based on a specific European history and the values that flow from it."[30]

The Americans, of course, were perfectly content to go to war in 1999 without UN authorization; indeed, many in the Clinton administration hoped it would set a useful precedent. As the British political scientist Christopher Croker notes, " 'Multilateral if possible, unilateral if necessary' was the catechism of the Clinton administration."[31] Throughout the war itself, the American commander, General Wesley Clark, like most of his American colleagues, expressed a certain impatient disdain for the Europeans' "legal issues." As de Villepin rightly recalls, the Americans, along with Tony Blair's Britain, saw Kosovo "as the first instance of a customary right to intervene on humanitarian grounds without a UN mandate. We, however, saw it as an exception, justified by wide support and the threat of an imminent humanitarian disaster."[32]

But exceptions can be deadly, especially with something as fragile and often violated as international law concerning the use of force. The fact remained that the Kosovo war was illegal, and not only because it lacked Security Council authorization. Serbia was a sovereign state that had not committed aggression against another state, but was simply slaughtering its own ethnic Albanian population. The intervention, therefore, violated a cardinal principle, perhaps *the* cardinal principle, of the UN Charter: the inviolable sovereign equality of all

[30] Cooper, *The Breaking of Nations,* p. 61.

[31] Croker, *Empires in Conflict:* 3.

[32] De Villepin, "Law, Force and Justice," speech delivered at the International Institute for Strategic Studies, March 27, 2003.

nations.[33] That has been the bedrock principle of international law for centuries. The seventeenth-century legal theorist Hugo Grotius had declared the principle of nonintervention the sine qua non of any system of international law. The so-called Westphalian system erected after the devastating religious wars of the mid-seventeenth century enshrined national sovereignty and the principle of noninterference as the prerequisites for international peace. Over the next three centuries, to be sure, the Westphalian system was a bit of a fraud: It is hard to name a single year in the last three centuries when some nation was not interfering in another nation's internal affairs. Still, the principle and theory underlying it were logical if not practicable. For if national sovereignty is not held sacred, and each nation's own sense of justice and morality may lead it to intervene in another country, on what foundation could any legal order be established? Would every nation be its own judge of right and wrong? At the time of the Kosovo conflict, Henry Kissinger warned that "the abrupt abandonment of the concept of national sovereignty" risked a world unmoored from any notion of order, legal or otherwise. "Once the doctrine of universal intervention spreads and competing truths con-

---

[33] Some might point to the Convention on Genocide as providing some legal justification for the war, but the Convention stipulated that nations must "call upon the competent organs of the United Nations" to take such action "under the Charter of the United Nations as they consider appropriate for the prevention and suppression of acts of genocide." Nations were not supposed to undertake such actions on their own or even in large groups. NATO was not conceived as a substitute for the legal authority of the UN.

test, we risk entering a world in which, in G. K. Chesterton's phrase, 'virtue runs amok.' "[34]

But many Europeans at the time rejected this complaint. Robert Cooper, writing in response to Kissinger, has argued that postmodern Europe is "no longer a zone of competing truths." The end of the Cold War has produced "a common set of values in Europe," and these common values have made "postmodern intervention sustainable both morally and practically *in the European context*."[35] In 1999, just four years before the Iraq war, Europeans did not believe international legitimacy resided exclusively at the UN Security Council, or in the UN Charter, or even in the traditional principles of international law, but in common moral values.

Some legal scholars have argued that the Kosovo war was perhaps legal according to an evolving standard of international law that treats imminent human catastrophe as an exception to the rule of nonintervention. But this is the triumph of morality over law. Taking such action in Kosovo, without Security Council approval, left the determination of international justice in the hands of a relatively small number of powerful Western nations. Is that a rules-based system?

It may be worth noting that in reaching its moral conclusion in 1999, Europe did not speak "in the name of peoples." Most of the nations of Latin America, Africa, and the

[34] Henry Kissinger, "The End of NATO as We Know It?", *The Washington Post*, August 15, 1999, B7.

[35] Cooper, *The Breaking of Nations*, pp. 60–61. Emphasis added. "Postmodern intervention" outside the European context, it has become clear, is another matter.

Arab world vigorously objected to the abrogation of the UN Charter in Kosovo, no doubt fearing, correctly, that Western liberal principles of moral responsibility could someday be employed to justify intervention against them. The nations of the North and West thus divided sharply from the nations of the South and East, and, as Michael Glennon has noted, "on the most fundamental of issues: namely, when armed intervention is appropriate." If anything, the Kosovo war demonstrated that "although the UN's rules purport to represent a single global view—indeed, universal law—on when and whether force can be justified, the UN's members (not to mention their populations) are clearly not in agreement."[36]

Glennon, an international legal scholar, has argued that the principle of nonintervention embodied in the UN Charter has been violated so many times over the past six decades that it can no longer qualify as international law; in legal parlance it has fallen into a state of "desuetude." Whether one accepts this view or not, it is certainly true that when the United States and some of its allies went to war against Saddam Hussein in March 2003, the principle that the UN Security Council alone could authorize the use of force had not been established, not even by the Europeans themselves. Secretary of State Colin Powell could well argue, as he did in October 2002, that the United States and its supporters possessed the "authority to intervene in Iraq . . . just as we did in Kosovo." As Glennon notes, the UN Charter "does not permit humani-

[36] Michael J. Glennon, "Why the Security Council Failed," *Foreign Affairs*, Vol. 82, Iss. 3, May/June 2003.

tarian intervention any more than it does preventive war."[37] In 2003 France and Germany and other European nations were demanding that the United States adhere to an international legal standard that they themselves had ignored, for sound moral and humanitarian reasons, a mere four years earlier.

As the Iraq crisis approached in 2002 and early 2003, many Europeans simply shifted their view of both international law and international legitimacy. Legal scholars might have been working toward establishing new principles to justify humanitarian intervention. But European leaders, knowing well that such principles could be stretched to fit many circumstances, wanted to close all the loopholes. European leaders scuttled away from the moralistic principles they had used to justify war in Kosovo and began demanding a much more rigid adherence to the UN Charter. Joschka Fischer's *volte face* was the most striking, for when confronted by the American invasion of Iraq, Fischer categorically rejected the idea that armed intervention and the violation of a nation's sovereignty could *ever* be justified, even "in cases of gross human rights violations." If intervention in another nation's affairs was to become "the new principle," Fischer now warned, echoing the very arguments made by Kissinger in 1999, "there are numerous candidates.... When will [this principle] be applied? By whom will it be legitimized?"[38] Good questions all. But they were good questions in 1999, too.

[37] Michael J. Glennon, "Why the Security Council Failed," *Foreign Affairs,* Vol. 82, Iss. 3, May/June 2003.

[38] Fischer interview, *Die Zeit*, May 8, 2003.

The double standard Europeans applied in the cases of Kosovo and Iraq reveals more than a simple desire to uphold the principles of international law and enshrine the primacy of the Security Council. Javier Solana today insists that Europe's demand for a "rules-based approach" to international affairs "is not a ploy to constrain the U.S.," but surely it is at least partly that.[39]

The controversy over the American invasion of Iraq needs to be viewed in light of this recent history. UN Secretary General Kofi Annan has denounced America's "lawless use of force."[40] But four years ago, in the case of Kosovo, Annan himself articulated a noble principle of humanitarian intervention that placed humanitarian concerns above long-standing international legal traditions.[41] Jacques Chirac has accused the United States of having "undermined the multilateral system," insisting "no one can accept the anarchy of a society without rules."[42] But Chirac was willing to bend those rules in the name of defending Kosovo Albanians from slaughter. Europeans will protest that Kosovo and Iraq were different. Indeed they were. But any "rules-based" international order must apply the same sets of rules to different situations. Otherwise we return to a world where nations individually or in groups decide for themselves when war is and is not justified, guided by their own morality and sense of justice and order.

[39] Solana, "The Future of Transatlantic Relations: Reinvention or Reform?"

[40] Dana Milbank, "At UN, Bush Is Criticized Over Iraq," *The Washington Post*, September 24, 2003, A1.

[41] See Kofi A. Annan, "Two Concepts of Sovereignty," *The Economist*, September 18, 1999.

[42] Milbank, "At UN, Bush Is Criticized Over Iraq."

In fact that is the world we live in, and the only world we have ever lived in. It is a world where those with power, believing they have right on their side, impose their sense of justice on others. This simple reality of international existence is often described simplistically as "might makes right." But are all claims to justice and morality equally valid? The modern liberal, whether residing in Europe or in the United States, does not and cannot believe that, for liberalism has at its core a conviction about justice and morality, defined as the protection of the rights of the individual, without which liberalism itself is meaningless. During World War II, the allied democracies' claim to morality and justice was stronger than that of Hitler's Germany and Imperial Japan. During the Cold War, the liberal West's claim to morality and justice was stronger than that of the Soviet bloc. During the Kosovo war, NATO's claim to morality and justice was stronger than that of Slobodan Milosevic and Boris Yeltsin's Russia. The point is this: A world without a universal standard of international law need not be a world without morality and justice. Indeed, in the real world, the too-rigid application of the principles of international law can impede the pursuit of morality and justice, as the Europeans recognized in the case of Kosovo.

These days most Europeans argue, as do some Americans, that by invading Iraq without the Security Council's approval, the United States has "torn the fabric of the international order." But if there ever was an international order of the kind they describe, then Europe undermined it in 1999, too. In fact, the fabric of this hoped-for international order has yet to be knit.

The point here is not to catch Europeans contradicting themselves. If there has been a certain convenient flexibility in Europeans' definition of what constitutes "legitimacy" in recent years, it is because "legitimacy" is a genuinely elusive and mobile concept. Discovering where legitimacy lies at any given moment in history is an art, not a science reducible to the reading of international legal documents. For modern liberalism, of the kind that animates Americans and Europeans alike, Kosovo, Iraq, and innumerable other international crises of recent years have shown that the search for legitimacy constantly stumbles across a fundamental dilemma that is endemic to both liberalism and liberal internationalism.

The problem is that the modern liberal vision of progress in international affairs has always been bifocal.[43] On the one hand, liberalism has since the Enlightenment entertained a vision of a world peace based on an ever-strengthening international legal system. The success of such a system, however, depends on recognizing the inviolable sovereign equality of all nations, whether big or small, democratic or tyrannical, humane or barbarous. For as Grotius, Hans Morgenthau, and many others have asked, what international law could survive if states may violate one another's sovereignty in the interest of propagating democracy or human rights or any other moral good?

[43] The following discussion of liberalism and international law owes much to the work of Thomas L. Pangle and Peter J. Ahrensdorf in their book, *Justice Among Nations: On the Moral Basis of Power and Peace* (Lawrence, Kansas, 1999.)

On the other hand, modern liberalism has also cherished the rights and liberties of the individual, and has defined human progress as providing greater and greater protection to these rights and liberties across the globe. But in the absence of a sudden global democratic and liberal transformation, that goal can only be achieved by compelling tyrannical or barbarous regimes to behave more democratically and humanely, and sometimes, as in Kosovo, by force. Liberals have also believed, at least since Kant and Montesquieu, that tyrannical regimes tend to be more aggressive and warlike and therefore that global peace ultimately depends not on law but on the spread of political and commercial liberalism.[44] Even modern liberals of a more pragmatic bent have considered interference just and proper under certain circumstances. Thus Edmund Burke wrote after the horrors of the French Revolution, "A more mischievous idea cannot exist than that any degree of wickedness, violence and oppression may prevail in a Country, that the most abominable, murderous and exterminatory Rebellions may rage in it, or the most atrocious and bloody tyranny may domineer, and that no neighboring power can take cognizance of either, or afford succor to the miserable sufferers." Englishmen ought to be the last to insist upon a principle of noninterference, Burke argued, for England owed "its Laws and Liberties . . . to the contrary principle."[45]

[44] Both Kant and Montesquieu believed peace would be based primarily on the rise of commercialism in liberal nations, which would make them unwilling to fight one another.

[45] Letter to Lord Grenville of August 18, 1792, in Harvey C. Mans-

Kofi Annan, looking back on Kosovo, the genocide in Rwanda, and other crises, framed the modern liberal's crisis of legitimacy well. "On the one hand," he asked, "is it legitimate for a regional organization to use force without a UN mandate? On the other, is it permissible to let gross and systematic violations of human rights, with grave humanitarian consequences, continue unchecked?" Annan called the international community's inability "to reconcile these two compelling interests" a "tragedy." But the UN Secretary-General himself discovered no answer to this dilemma, other than to plead with the "international community" to find "consensus."[46]

Given the tension between these two liberal visions, however, what constitutes international legitimacy must always be a matter of dispute within the liberal, democratic world. Kant's vision of "perpetual peace" solved the problem, in theory, by presuming that all the nations in his imagined international system would be free, liberal republics. But the UN Charter, in practice, ignored Kant's prescription and enshrined the "sovereign equality of all its members," regardless of the nature of their governments.[47] The present international legal structure, therefore, does not and arguably cannot conform to liberalism's goal of ameliorating the human condition and securing the rights of all. As Robert Cooper notes, the

---

field Jr., *Selected Letters of Edmund Burke* (Chicago, 1984); Pangle and Ahrensdorf, *Justice Among Nations,* pp. 184–85.

46 See Annan, "Two Concepts of Sovereignty."

47 See Fukuyama, *The End of History and the Last Man,* pp. 281–82.

United Nations was meant "to defend the status quo and not to create a new order."[48]

All modern liberals must wrestle with this dilemma. For Europeans it is a particularly difficult problem. For Europe itself is the Kantian miracle; it has moved beyond the Westphalian order into a postmodern, supranational order. Ironically, while many Europeans now claim to define international legitimacy as strict obedience to the UN Charter and the Security Council, the European Union transcends the UN's exclusive focus on national sovereignty. It is all about interference. As a confederation of free states, the EU is more the fulfillment of Kant's liberal vision than of Grotius's. The "new postmodern European order," Cooper argues, "is based on entirely different ideas" than those on which the United Nations was based.[49] Tony Blair argued at the time of the Kosovo war that Europe must fight "for a new internationalism where the brutal repression of ethnic groups will not be tolerated [and] for a world where those responsible for crimes will have nowhere to hide."[50] If this is the "new internationalism," then the "old internationalism" of the UN Charter is

[48] Cooper, *The Breaking of Nations*, p. 58.

[49] Ibid.

[50] Tony Blair speech to the Chicago Chambers of Commerce, September 1998; Cooper, *The Breaking of Nations*, pp. 59–60. Nor have Europeans limited themselves in such intrusions on national sovereignty to their own continent. The International Criminal Court, which European governments championed, authorizes action against leaders and officials of other nations, even where those nations have not ratified the treaty.

dead. Europeans may have to choose which version of liberal internationalism they really intend to pursue. But whether they choose or not, they must at least recognize that the two paths diverge.

If the United States seeks legitimacy, which of these liberal visions should it aspire to follow? The United States is and always has been less divided on this question than Europeans are today. By nature, tradition, and ideology the United States has always tended toward the promotion of liberal principles in disregard of Westphalian niceties. Like Burke's England, the United States owes its existence, its "Laws and Liberties," to the principle of interference. Nor does the United States depend on a system of international laws as does the European Union, which is itself a structure of international laws. So it is not surprising, despite the American role in inventing the United Nations and drafting the UN Charter, that the United States has never fully accepted the UN's legitimacy, and least of all the UN Charter's doctrine of the inviolable sovereign equality of all nations. The United States has always been acutely jealous of its own sovereignty, but throughout the Cold War, and indeed throughout its history, the United States has been a good deal less concerned about the sovereign inviolability of other nations. It has reserved to itself the right to intervene anywhere and everywhere— from Latin America and the Caribbean to North Africa and the Middle East, from the South Pacific to East Asia and, finally, in the twentieth century, even in Europe. And although the United States is as capable of self-serving hypocrisy as other nations, it has generally justified intervention in the name of defending or spreading the cause of liberalism. During the Cold War, and much to the dismay of realist thinkers and statesmen from Morgenthau and Kennan to Kissinger, Americans were never willing to accept the legitimacy of the Soviet Union and constantly sought ways to undermine it from within and from without, even at the risk of global instability. An "evil empire" can have no legitimacy and no inviolable rights as a sovereign nation.

The United States in this sense is and always has been a revolutionary power, a sometimes unwitting but nevertheless persistent disturber of the status quo wherever its influence has grown. From the founding generation onward, Americans have looked at foreign tyrannies as transient, destined to topple before the forces of republicanism unleashed by America's own revolution. Even allied dictatorships have been regarded as inherently illegitimate;[51] hostile tyrannies have always been considered fair game. And if most Americans have been oblivious to their own nation's revolutionary impact on the world, the rest of the world has not been. John Quincy Adams, writing from London in 1817, observed, "The universal feeling of Europe in witnessing the gigantic growth of our population and power is that we shall, if united, become a very dangerous member of the society of nations."[52] In the early nineteenth century it was European conservatives

[51] The list of "friendly" dictators ultimately toppled with the connivance of the United States is long. Consider the fates of Ferdinand Marcos, Anastasio Somoza, Manuel Noriega, and the military junta of South Korea, to name a few.

[52] Letter to William Plumer, January 17, 1817, in Worthington Chauncey Ford, ed., *Writings of John Quincy Adams*, Vol. VI, (New York, 1968), p. 143; Lockey, *Pan-Americanism*, p. 159.

like Metternich who feared that the American Revolution, and the French upheaval it helped spark, would ripple outward and fatally engulf their institutions and society. Today it is the forces of conservatism in the Muslim world—the militant fundamentalists—who fear and seek to repel America's corrosive influence. And Europeans, consumed with carrying out radical changes on their own continent, seek stability and predictability in the world beyond. To these Europeans, the United States has once again become a dangerous member of the society of nations.

FAREWELL, WESTPHALIA

That danger, for Europeans, is encapsulated in the so-called Bush doctrine, with its declaration of confrontation with a global "axis of evil." Many Europeans and some Americans profess themselves shocked that the United States would announce its intention to seek "regime change" in despotic governments, and if necessary at the expense of international law and the UN Charter. But in the light of American history, especially that of the previous half century, could anything be less shocking? The Bush doctrine, such as it is, has sprung naturally out of the liberal, revolutionary American tradition. Does anyone imagine that Harry Truman and Dean Acheson, John F. Kennedy and Ronald Reagan, or for that matter Theodore Roosevelt, Woodrow Wilson, and Franklin Roosevelt, or even Bill Clinton, would have objected to the idea that hostile third world tyrants seeking weapons of mass destruction should be removed by force, with or without Security Council authorization?[53] The United States has many times toppled tyrannical regimes with less provocation, and less obvious justification. If the liberal vision of securing the rights of all peoples may run afoul of international legal traditions and of the UN Security Council, it should come as no surprise that a liberal nation, such as the United States, might be even more inclined to set aside legal and institutional constraints when it is a matter of defending its own citizens and soil against dictators with deadly arsenals.

Today the problem of legitimacy has been made a good deal more complex by the fact that the emergence of a unipolar era coincided with two other evolving historical phenomena, the increasing proliferation of weapons of mass destruction and the rise of international terrorism—both of which these days seem more threatening to Americans than they do to Europeans. It has been the Bush administration's response to these phenomena, including the so-called doctrine of pre-emption, that has caused the greatest uproar on both sides of the Atlantic.[54]

[53] Bill Clinton, in fact, argued in July 2003 that seeking "regime change" in Iraq was the correct policy if Saddam Hussein did not disarm. Bill Clinton interview on CNN, July 22, 2003.

[54] The term "pre-emption" is not an accurate description of the Bush administration's doctrine. It implies taking action against a nation or group that is about to strike. What the Bush administration did in Iraq was "prevention," which implies taking action even before the decision to strike has been taken by a potentially hostile power, and perhaps well before. This is the harder case from a traditional international legal point of view. For the purposes of this essay, I will use the term "preventive" war.

Many Europeans, and many others around the world, insist the American willingness to take preventive action is the prime example of the superpower's disregard for international law and international order, the epitome of America's new illegitimacy. "Until now," UN Secretary-General Kofi Annan asserts, "it has been understood that when States go beyond [immediate self-defense], and decide to use force to deal with broader threats to international peace and security, they need the unique legitimacy provided by the United Nations." The very "logic" of preventive war, therefore, poses "a fundamental challenge to the principles on which, however imperfectly, world peace and stability have rested for the last fifty-eight years."[55] Set aside for the moment Annan's rendition of the history of the Cold War, with its erroneous assertion that Americans and Europeans accepted the "unique legitimacy" of the United Nations throughout those decades, or even in 1999. The more interesting question is whether new international circumstances have forced not just the United States but also Europeans, and even Kofi Annan himself, to reexamine traditional international legal principles and definitions of "legitimacy."

The idea of preventive war is not new, of course. As Robert Cooper notes, the Bush administration's notion of preventive war is not fundamentally different from "the longstanding British doctrine that no single power should be allowed to dominate the continent of Europe," a principle that justified the launching of the War of the Spanish

[55] Milbank, "At U.N., Bush is Criticized Over Iraq."

Succession in the late seventeenth century.[56] Nor is prevention a novel concept in the modern era. John F. Kennedy threatened preventive action in the Cuban Missile Crisis. In the mid-1980s, following the bombing of the Marine barracks in Beirut, Secretary of State George P. Shultz publicly called for a doctrine of preventive action against international terrorism—and, one might add, with no public outcry from Europe.

Even before the Bush administration publicly enunciated a policy of preventive war in 2002, moreover, there had been a growing body of opinion in the United States, and even in Europe, that preventive action might at times be necessary to meet new international threats, regardless of the fact that such action violated traditional notions of international law and the principles of the Westphalian system. In the United States, it was the renowned liberal just war theorist, Michael Walzer, who argued in 1998 that traditional legal arguments against preventive war looked "different when the danger is posed by weapons of mass destruction, which are developed in secret, and which might be used suddenly, without warning, with catastrophic results." Not only might preventive action be "legitimate" under such circumstances, Walzer argued, with Iraq specifically in mind. But so would "unilateral action" without a Security Council authorization. The "refusal of a U.N. majority to act forcefully" was not "a good reason for ruling out the use of force by any member state that can use it effectively." If Americans were not

[56] Cooper, *The Breaking of Nations*, p. 64.

not ready sometimes to "act unilaterally," Walzer concluded, then "we are not ready for real life in international society."[57]

From the opposite end of the ideological spectrum, Henry Kissinger, the great proponent of the principles of national sovereignty, noninterference, and the sanctity of the Westphalian system, nevertheless argued that such principles now had to be set aside in order to confront changed international circumstances. "The international regimen following the Treaty of Westphalia," Kissinger argued before the invasion of Iraq, "was based on the concept of an impermeable nation-state and a limited military technology which generally permitted a nation to run the risk of awaiting an unambiguous challenge." In the post–Cold War era, however, "the terrorist threat transcends the nation-state," and the proliferation of weapons of mass destruction had made the risk of waiting too great.[58] When Henry Kissinger makes such a pronouncement, the Westphalian system is no more. In fact, the twin dangers of weapons proliferation and terrorism are forcing many to reevaluate both the legality and the legitimacy of the use of preventive force. Javier Solana insists that "the fight against international terrorism . . . has to take place within the rules of international law," but is that possible without significant changes in the rules themselves?[59]

[57] Michael Walzer, "The Hard Questions: Lone Ranger," *The New Republic*, April 27, 1998.

[58] Henry Kissinger, "Iraq Poses Most Consequential Foreign-Policy Decision for Bush," *Los Angeles Times*, August 8, 2002.

[59] Glenn Kessler, "Bush: Israel Must Defend Itself," *The Washington Post*, October 7, 2003, A19.

Robert Cooper, who happens to be one of Solana's top advisers, acknowledges that in a world of proliferating weapons of mass destruction, "following well-established legal norms and relying on self-defense will not solve the problem."[60] And even Kofi Annan has suggested that UN members should begin considering "criteria for an early authorization of coercive measures to address certain types of threats—for instance, terrorist groups armed with weapons of mass destruction."[61] If the United States fears for its safety and wants to take preventive action, Annan is suggesting, it could seek UN Security Council authority for a preventive strike.

Annan's proposal, whatever its practicality, reveals a core truth about international attitudes toward prevention. The real issue may not be prevention itself but who is doing the preventing, and who gets to decide when and where preventive war occurs. In this as in many other cases, what Europeans object to is not so much American actions, but what they consider the "unilateralism" of American actions. The dispute over preventive war is really little more than a recapitulation of the central unipolar predicament: How will the sole superpower be controlled?

[60] Cooper, *The Breaking of Nations*, p. 64.

[61] Kofi Annan speech to the UN General Assembly, September 22, 2003.

WHAT IS "MULTILATERALISM"?

Most Europeans would argue that if the United States seeks to gain international legitimacy for any use of force, it must avoid acting "unilaterally" and must embrace a foreign policy of "multilateralism." And most Americans would gladly agree—so long as they did not look too closely at what Europeans mean by the term. For when Americans speak of "multilateralism," they mean a policy that actively solicits and gains the support of allies. For most Americans, even those who proclaim themselves "multilateralists," a UN Security Council authorization is always desirable but never essential—"multilateral if possible, unilateral if necessary." It is a means to the end of gaining allied support. It is not, for the vast majority of Americans, an end in itself.

But when Europeans speak of "multilateralism" these days, the term has a much more formal and legalistic cast. To Europeans it means gaining legitimate sanction from duly constituted international bodies before undertaking any action and indeed as an essential prerequisite for action. A recent poll showed a majority of Americans willing to bypass the UN Security Council if America's "vital interests" were threatened. But in the same poll a majority of Europeans insisted that they would abide by a decision of the Security Council even if it meant sacrificing their nation's vital interests.[62]

At least that is what Europeans say today, after the Iraq

[62] See *Transatlantic Trends 2003*.

war. In 1999, when the issue was Kosovo, Europeans felt differently. Once again, it turns out that even for Europeans, with their legalistic, principled understanding of the term, the attempt to define international legitimacy simply as "multilateralism" founders on the same shifting sands as all other simple definitions. For what is "multilateralism"? If it does not mean strict obedience to the UN Security Council, and in 1999 it did not, then "multilateralism" becomes a slippery concept.

What, exactly, made American action in Iraq "unilateral"? The United States, after all, did not act alone in invading Iraq in March 2003 but had a number of international partners, including such prominent members of the European Union as Great Britain, Spain, and Poland. The American action was "multilateral" in some sense, therefore, even without a UN authorization, just as the Kosovo war was "multilateral" despite the lack of Security Council approval. Nor would Europeans have denounced American action in Iraq as "unilateral" had France, Germany, and Great Britain all agreed to support the war but Russia and China had opposed it—just as Europeans did not condemn their own war in Kosovo as "unilateral" just because Russia and much of the developing world were opposed. De Villepin acknowledges that "some powers in the South" opposed the war in Kosovo. The war was nevertheless justified, de Villepin argues, by the "wide support" it enjoyed in Europe.[63] As Cooper suggests, Europeans considered that their near unanimous support for

[63] De Villepin, "Law, Force, and Justice," speech to the International Institute for Security Studies, March 27, 2003.

the war, based as it was on common European history and common European values, provided legitimacy enough. But should international legitimacy be defined as whatever Europeans can agree on?

In the case of the American invasion of Iraq, the Europeans erected a high international standard of legitimacy. "The authority of our action," Dominique de Villepin declared in his famous speech to the UN Security Council in February 2003, had to be based "on the unity of the international community."[64] But what does that mean? Was de Villepin arguing that no action could ever be taken without the unanimous consent of the entire international community? Or is "unity" another word that needs to be defined loosely? The United States had the support of dozens of nations for its war in Iraq, but according to de Villepin and many other Europeans, not enough. Is there then a certain, magic number of supporting nations that bestows legitimacy? Or is it the quality of one's allies that matters more than the quantity when defining "multilateralism"? Is France worth more than Spain? "Legitimacy depends on creating a wide international consensus," Javier Solana insists. But how wide is wide? And who will decide when it is wide enough?[65] The answers to such questions are inevitably subjective, and far too subjective to serve as the underpinning of any "rules-based" international order.

[64] De Villepin statement to the UN Security Council, February 14, 2003.

[65] Solana, "The Future of Transatlantic Relations: Reinvention or Reform?" *Progressive Governance*, July 10, 2003.

It is difficult to avoid the conclusion that when Europeans, and Americans, claim that American action in Iraq was "unilateral," they do not really mean that the United States lacked wide international support. They mean the United States lacked wide European support. The problem was not that Russia and China were opposed—when did any American or European ever worry about that? Nor was it that the vast majority of nations in Africa, Latin America, and the Middle East were opposed. For much of the past century, the majority of the world's population has opposed many American policies, and many European policies, too, without causing a crisis of legitimacy in the West. No, what the critics mean by America's "unilateralism" in the Iraq war was that the United States did not have the full support of all its traditional European allies, including, most spectacularly, France and Germany. The Bush administration was "unilateralist" not because it lost the support of Moscow, Beijing, São Paolo, Kuala Lumpur, and dozens of other capitals, but because it lost the support of Paris and Berlin.

In the end, moreover, what critics really mean by American "unilateralism" is not that the United States acted alone, but that it would not and could not be constrained, even by its closest friends. From the perspective of Berlin and Paris, the United States was "unilateralist" because no European power had any real influence over it. As Joschka Fischer most candidly put it, "The question now is: What will become of the Europeans given the dominant role of the United States? Will they be able to determine their own fate or will they merely be forced to carry out what has been decided elsewhere?" Yes, the

British and Spaniards supported the United States in Iraq, Fischer acknowledges, but "the decisive question" was whether these countries "can have or ever did have any influence at all."[66] Thus, even if there were one hundred nations on America's side, and even if three-quarters of European nations supported American action, it is the loss of influence over the United States that makes American policy "unilateral."

That is why many Europeans have found so objectionable the Bush administration's references to "coalitions of the willing" as the foreign policy tool of choice for the United States in the future, rather than institutionalized alliances such as NATO. The idea that "the mission determines the coalition" frees the United States from all obligations and from European influence, even if some Europeans are part of the coalition. It is also why many Europeans found so troubling American talk of "old" and "new" Europe; it was viewed as an American strategy of divide-and-conquer, a way of further minimizing the influence of a united Europe, if such a thing were ever to come into existence.

As Javier Solana puts it, "Most of us would prefer to be called an 'ally' or a 'partner' rather than a 'tool' in a box." If the United States will once again consider itself bound to its European allies, Solana suggests, the Europeans will in turn provide it the support and legitimacy it needs. "Treat your friends like allies and they will behave like allies," Javier Solana has argued since the Iraq war. "They allow

[66] Fischer interview, *Die Zeit*, May 8, 2003.

for and legitimize leadership."[67] And although Solana again insists that Europeans in demanding this treatment are not seeking a "de facto European veto on American initiatives," of course they are. No one can blame them for wanting such a veto. Still, when all is said and done, the crisis of legitimacy today is not only about principles of law, or even about the supreme authority of the UN Security Council. It is also very much the product of a transatlantic struggle for influence. It is Europe's response to the unipolar predicament.

THE LEGITIMACY OF LIBERALISM

It would be tempting for Americans, therefore, to dismiss the whole issue of legitimacy as a ruse and a fraud. During the 2000 presidential campaign, George W. Bush's top foreign policy adviser, Condoleezza Rice, derided the belief, which she attributed to the Clinton administration, "that the support of many states—or even better, of institutions like the United Nations—is essential to the legitimate exercise of power." But as it turns out, even the Bush administration felt compelled to seek European approval for its action, and at the place where Europeans insisted approval be granted, the UN Security Council. Perhaps the Bush administration did not need France and Germany, but it believed it needed the support at least of

[67] Javier Solana, "The Future of Transatlantic Relations: Reinvention or Reform?" *Progressive Governance*, July 10, 2003.

Great Britain. Why? Not because British troops were essential to the success of the invasion of Iraq. It was the patina of international legitimacy Blair's support provided—a legitimacy that the American people wanted and needed, as Bush officials well understood. Nor can there be any question that the Bush administration has suffered from its failure to gain the full approval of Europe, and thus a broader international legitimacy, for the invasion of Iraq—and suffered at home as well as abroad.

There are sound reasons why the United States needs European approval, reasons unrelated to international law, the strength of the Security Council, and the as-yet-nonexistent "fabric of the international order." Europe matters because Europe and the United States remain the heart of the liberal, democratic world. The liberal, democratic essence of the United States makes it difficult if not impossible for Americans to ignore the fears, concerns, interests, and demands of its fellow liberal democracies. American foreign policy will be drawn by American liberalism to seek greater harmony with Europe, *if* Europeans are willing and able to make such harmony possible.

The alternative course will be difficult for the United States to sustain, for it is questionable whether the United States can operate effectively over time without the moral support and approval of the democratic world. This is not for the reasons usually cited. While most American advocates of "multilateralism" have focused on the need for the material cooperation of allies, it is America's need for international legitimacy, defined as the approval of the liberal, democratic world—represented, above all, by Europe—that will in the end prove more decisive in shaping America's course.[68] Whether the United States can "go it alone" in a material sense is an open question. Militarily, it can and does go virtually alone, even when the Europeans are fully on board, as in Kosovo and in the first Persian Gulf war. Economically, it can go alone in the reconstruction of places like Iraq if it absolutely has to—five decades ago, after all, it reconstructed Europe and Japan with its own funds. But whether the American people will continually be willing and able to support both military actions and the burdens of postwar occupations in the face of constant charges of illegitimacy by its closest democratic allies—that is more doubtful.

Americans have always cared what the rest of the world thinks of them, or at least what the liberal world thinks. Their reputation for insularity and indifference is undeserved. Americans were told to care by the founding generation—in their Declaration of Independence, Americans declared the importance of having a "decent respect for the opinion of mankind," by which they meant Europe. Ever since, Americans have been forced to care what the liberal world thinks by their unique national ideology. For unlike the nationalisms of Europe, American nationalism is not rooted in blood and soil; it is a universalist

---

[68] It is not yet the case that the world's other major liberal democracies, including India and Japan, weigh as heavily in American calculations as does Europe. Whether this is because they are relative newcomers to "the West" or because of cultural and racial prejudices in the transatlantic community is hard to say. But the views of New Delhi do not carry as much weight, or excite as much passion, as the views of Paris.

ideology that binds Americans together. Americans for much of the past three centuries have considered themselves the vanguard of a worldwide liberal revolution. Their foreign policy from the beginning has not been only about defending and promoting their material national interests. "We fight not just for ourselves but for all mankind," Benjamin Franklin declared at America's War of Independence, and whether or not that has always been true, most Americans have always wanted to believe it was true. There can be no clear dividing line between the domestic and the foreign, therefore, and no clear distinction between what the democratic world thinks about America and what Americans think about themselves. Every profound foreign policy debate in America's history, from the time when Jefferson squared off against Hamilton, has ultimately been a debate about the nation's identity and has posed for Americans the primal question: "Who are we?" Because Americans do care, the steady denial of international legitimacy by fellow democracies will over time become debilitating and perhaps even paralyzing.

Americans therefore cannot ignore the unipolar predicament. Perhaps the singular failure of the Bush administration may have been that it has been too slow to recognize this. Bush and his advisers came to office guided by the narrow realism that dominated in Republican foreign policy circles during the Clinton years. The Clinton administration, Condoleezza Rice wrote in a famous essay in January 2000, had failed to focus on the "national interest" and instead had addressed itself to " 'humanitarian interests' or the interests of 'the international community.'" The Bush administration, by contrast, would take a fresh look at all treaties, obligations, and alliances and reevaluate them in terms of America's "national interest."[69]

The notion that the United States could take such a narrow view of its "national interest" has always been mistaken. Americans had "humanitarian interests" before the term was invented. But besides being an analytical error, the enunciation of this "realist" approach by the sole superpower in a unipolar era was a serious foreign policy error. The global hegemon cannot proclaim to the world that it will be guided only by its own definition of its "national interest." For this is precisely what even America's closest friends fear, that the United States will wield its unprecedented vast power only for itself. In her essay, Rice derided "the belief that the United States is exercising power legitimately only when it is doing so on behalf of someone or something else." But for the rest of the world, what other source of legitimacy can there be? When the United States acts in its own interests, Rice claimed, as would many Americans, it necessarily serves the interests of everyone. "To be sure," Rice argued, "there is nothing wrong with doing something that benefits all humanity, but that is, in a sense, a second-order effect."[70] But could even America's closest friends ever be persuaded that an America always pursuing its self-interest can be relied upon to serve their interests, too, as some kind of "second-order effect"?

[69] Condoleezza Rice, "Promoting the National Interest," *Foreign Affairs,* 79 (January/February 2000): 47.
[70] Ibid.

Both the unipolar predicament and the American character require a much more expansive definition of American interests. The United States can neither appear to be acting only in its self-interest, nor can it in fact act as if its own national interest were all that mattered. In the words of the oft-quoted Jewish sage Hillel, "If I am not for myself, who will be for me? If I am not for others, what am I?" The United States must, indeed, act in ways that benefit all humanity, as it has frequently tried to do in the past, and it must certainly seek to benefit that part of humanity that shares America's liberal principles. Even at times of dire emergency, and perhaps especially at those times, the world's sole superpower needs to demonstrate that it wields its great power on behalf of its principles and all who share them.

The manner in which the United States conducts itself in Iraq today is especially important in this regard. At stake is not only the future of Iraq and the Middle East more generally, but also of America's reputation, its reliability, and its legitimacy as a world leader. The United States will be judged, and should be judged, by the care and commitment it takes to secure a democratic peace in Iraq. It will be judged by whether it indeed advances the cause of liberalism, in Iraq and elsewhere, or whether it merely defends its own interests.

No one has made this argument more powerfully, and more presciently, than that quintessential realist, Henry Kissinger. In the same essay where Kissinger made the case for moving beyond the Westphalian system, he also insisted that by leading this new, "revolutionary" approach the United States incurred "a special responsibility." Because of its power, and "precisely because of the precedent-setting nature of this war," Kissinger argued before the invasion, "its outcome will determine the way American actions will be viewed internationally." The task in Iraq, Kissinger argued, was not just to win the war but to "[convey] to the rest of the world that our first preemptive war has been imposed by necessity and that we seek the world's interests, not exclusively our own." America's "special responsibility, as the most powerful nation in the world, is to work toward an international system that rests on more than military power—indeed, that strives to translate power into cooperation. Any other attitude will gradually isolate and exhaust us."

The United States, in short, must pursue legitimacy in the manner truest to its nature, by promoting the principles of liberal democracy, not only as a means to greater security, but as an end in itself. Success in such endeavors will provide the United States a measure of legitimacy in the liberal, democratic world, and even in Europe. For Europeans cannot forever ignore their own vision of a more humane world, even if they are these days more preoccupied with their vision of a strengthened international legal order.

Nor can the United States, in promoting liberalism, fail to take the interests and the fears of its liberal democratic allies in Europe into account. The United States should try to fulfill its part of a new transatlantic bargain by granting Europeans some influence over the exercise of American power—if, that is, the Europeans in turn will wield that influence wisely. The NATO alliance—an alliance of and for liberal democracies—could be the locus of such a bargain, if there is to be one. NATO is where the United States has already ceded influence to Europeans, who vote on an equal footing with the superpower in all the alliance's deliberations. Indeed, NATO has for decades been the one organization capable of reconciling American hegemony with European autonomy and influence. And NATO even today retains a sentimental attraction for Americans, more potent than the attraction they feel for the United Nations.

But can the United States cede some power to Europe without putting American security, and indeed Europe's and the entire liberal democratic world's security, at risk in the process? Here lies the rub. For even with the best of intentions, the United States cannot enlist the cooperation of Europeans if there is no common assessment of the nature of global threats today, and of the means that must be employed to meet them. But it is precisely this gap in perception that has driven the United States and Europe apart in the post–Cold War world.

If it is true, as Robert Cooper suggests, that international legitimacy stems from shared values and a shared history, does such commonality still exist within the West now that the Cold War has ended? For while the liberal transatlantic community still shares much in common, the philosophical schism on the fundamental questions of world order may now be overwhelming those commonalities. It is hard to imagine the crisis of legitimacy being resolved so long as this schism persists. For even if the United States were to fulfill its part of the bargain, and grant the Europeans the influence they crave, would the Europeans, with their very different perception of the world, fulfill theirs? Were Europeans and Americans ever

to agree on the nature of the common threat, the cooperation they managed during the Cold War would not be
hard to resume. But so long as Europeans and Americans
do not share a common view of the threat posed by terrorism and weapons of mass destruction, they will not join in
a common strategy to meet those threats. Nor will
Europeans accord the United States legitimacy when it
seeks to address those threats by itself, and by what it
regards as sometimes the only means possible, by force.

And what, then, is the United States to do? Should
Americans, in the interest of transatlantic harmony, try to
alter their perceptions of global threats to match that of
their European friends? To do so would be irresponsible.
Not only American security but the security of the liberal
democratic world depends today, as it has depended for
the past half century, on American power. Kofi Annan
may convince himself that the relative peace and stability
the world has known since World War II was the product
of the UN Security Council and the UN Charter. But even
Europeans, in moments of clarity, know that is not true.
"The U.S. is the only truly global player," Joschka Fischer
has declared, "and I must warn against underestimating
its importance for peace and stability in the world. And
beware, too, of underestimating what the U.S. means for
our own security."[71]

But the United States has played that role not by
adopting Europe's postmodern worldview, but by seeing
the world through its own eyes. Were Americans now to
adopt the worldview of postmodern Europe, neither the

[71] Joschka Fischer interview, *Stern*, October 2, 2002.

United States nor postmodern Europe itself would long remain secure. Today, most Europeans believe the United States exaggerates the dangers in the world. After September 11, 2001, most Americans fear they haven't taken those dangers seriously enough.

Herein lies the tragedy. To address today's global threats Americans will need the legitimacy that Europe can provide. But Europeans may well fail to provide it. In their effort to constrain the superpower, they will lose sight of the mounting dangers in the world, dangers far greater than those posed by the United States. In their nervousness about unipolarity, they may forget the dangers of a multipolarity in which nonliberal and nondemocratic powers come to outweigh Europe in the global competition. In their passion for international legal order, they may lose sight of the other liberal principles that have made postmodern Europe what it is today. Europeans thus may succeed in debilitating the United States, but since they have no intention of supplementing American power with their own, the net result will be a diminution of the total amount of power that the liberal democratic world can bring to bear in its defense—and in defense of liberalism itself.

Right now many Europeans are betting that the risks from the "axis of evil," from terrorism and tyrants, will never be as great as the risk of an American Leviathan unbound. Perhaps it is in the nature of a postmodern Europe to make such a judgment. But now may be the time for the wisest heads in Europe, including those living in the birthplace of Pascal, to begin asking what will result if that wager proves wrong.